Mike Holt's Illustrated Guide to

ELECTRICAL ESTIMATING

2nd Edition

Mike Holt Enterprises, Inc.
888.NEC.CODE (632.2633) • www.MikeHolt.com • Info@MikeHolt.com

NOTICE TO THE READER

Mike Holt's Illustrated Guide to Electrical Estimating, 2nd Edition

Second Printing: September 2016

Technical Illustrator: Mike Culbreath
Cover Design: Madalina Iordache-Levay
Layout Design and Typesetting: Cathleen Kwas

ISBN 978-1-932685-50-3

Produced and Printed in the USA

For more information, call 888.NEC.CODE (632.2633), or e-mail Info@MikeHolt.com.

I dedicate this book to the
Lord Jesus Christ,
my mentor and teacher.
Proverbs 16:3

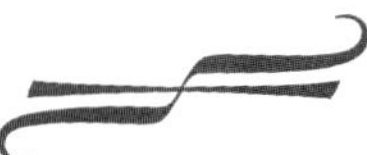

One Team

To Our Instructors and Students:

We're committed to providing you the finest product with the fewest errors, but we're realistic and know that there'll be errors found and reported after the printing of this book. The last thing we want is for you to have problems finding, communicating, or accessing this information. It's unacceptable to us for there to be even one error in our textbooks or answer keys. For this reason, we're asking you to work together with us as One Team.

Students: Please report any errors you may find to your instructor.

Instructors: Please communicate these errors to us by sending an e-mail to corrections@mikeholt.com.

Our Commitment:

We'll continue to list all of the corrections that come through for all of our textbooks and answer keys on our Website. The most up-to-date answer keys will always be available to instructors to download from our instructor Website. We don't want you to have problems finding this updated information, so we're outlining where to go for all of this below:

To view textbook and answer key corrections: Students and instructors go to our Website, www.MikeHolt.com, click on "Books" in the sidebar of links, and then click on "Corrections."

To download the most up-to-date answer keys: Instructors go to our Website, www.MikeHolt.com, click on "Instructors" in the sidebar of links and then click on "Answer Keys." On this page you'll find instructions for accessing and downloading these answer keys.

If you're not registered as an instructor you'll need to register. Your registration will be sent to our educational director who in turn will review and approve your registration. In your approval e-mail will be the login and password so you can have access to all of the answer keys. If you have a situation that needs immediate attention, please contact the office directly at 888.NEC.CODE (632.2633).

Call 888.NEC.CODE (632.2633) or visit us online at www.MikeHolt.com

Table of Contents

About This Textbook

Mike Holt's *Illustrated Guide to Electrical Estimating*

Congratulations on making the decision to learn estimating. This is a skill that can make or break a career, and make or break a company. Making an estimate isn't making "an educated guess." Estimating is a methodology with precise requirements. Learn those requirements, and you can be a good estimator.

An accurate estimate helps the different functions of a business in many ways. For example:

- The salesperson can bid correctly on a project, rather than lose money by underbidding or lose the project by overbidding.
- The salesperson can accurately explain the bid to the customer, and perhaps be the only bidder able to do so.
- The project manager can use that budget to plan and manage projects profitably.
- Crews can order from the bill of materials in the estimate, to keep work flowing without stockpiling costly materials "just in case."
- The company can manage cash flow much better. And cash flow is the lifeblood of every company.

To get these benefits, you must understand the concepts behind making an accurate estimate and what the methods are for arriving at the correct final numbers. This course gives you that understanding.

On the flip side, incorrect estimates can easily cause failed bids, failed projects, and cash flow crunches. A failed bid means you don't get the work. A failed project means you got the work, but lost money on the job and perhaps lost future business with the customer as well. A cash flow problem, if serious enough, can cause your company to go out of business.

By taking this course, you are on your way to avoiding those failures. And you are on the way to enjoying the benefits, to your company and to your career, of getting it right.

Estimating is a way of seeing, in advance, what you need to correctly complete a given project *profitably.* The costs include time, labor, and materials. If you know those costs and they are figured into your bid and price, then you can do the job itself correctly and profitably. You won't face the choice between cutting corners and breaking even. Instead, you'll be able to do the project to the quality standards you promised and your customer expects.

Many variables figure into an estimate. "Seat of the pants" estimates can't possibly account for all of these. But, a methodical approach to estimating does. And that prevents unpleasant surprises after the project is already under way.

In some cases, the estimate can reveal that your company shouldn't even take on this project. You can pass the disaster on to a competitor. You can't do every possible job that comes along, nor would you want to. With accurate estimates, you can bid on those projects that are the best fit for your company's resources and expertise and those projects that are the most profitable.

In this introduction, we've mentioned estimating and bidding as though they are separate things. That's because they are. The estimate is your tool for determining how much the job will cost. The bid is how much you want the job to pay. The difference between the two is your profit. If there's no difference, there's no profit.

We also mentioned that an accurate estimate helps you present the customer with an accurate bid. Bidding is a separate discipline, but it begins with an accurate estimate. You can win a bidding contest with an accurate bid, even if your bid isn't the lowest and in some cases even if it is the highest.

The reason for that is many bids are based on guesswork or the prices competitors charge rather than on the actual costs plus profit. If you can show a customer why your bid is accurate, the confidence in your bid and your ability to deliver the project without cost overruns goes up. That may not guarantee you'll get the job, but it does guarantee you'll know what you're getting into. And that is just one of the big benefits of making accurate estimates.

Scope of This Textbook

Electrical estimating is important to various individuals with different roles in the electrical industry. The apprentice and electrician need an understanding of estimating to gain a perspective for the value of their work. The aspiring estimator needs to understand the nuts and bolts of estimating to properly perform a complete and accurate estimate. The electrical contractor must know how to estimate to determine the job's selling price and to profitably manage that job once it is sold.

The primary purpose of this textbook is to help you understand the estimating and bidding processes. We will explain how to determine material cost, labor cost, and the calculation of direct job costs, overhead, and profit to complete the bid.

Mike Holt's *Illustrated Guide to Electrical Estimating* is divided into 9 chapters.

Chapter 1—Introduction. Chapter 1 explains the purpose, importance, and need for proper estimating.

Chapter 2—About Estimating. This chapter explains what estimating is all about—the good, the bad, and the ugly.

Chapter 3—Understanding Labor Units. Chapter 3 introduces labor units and explains what they are, how they are used, and how you can (and must) develop your own.

Chapter 4—The Estimating Process. In this chapter we will start with estimate preparation and end with extending and totaling material cost and labor hours.

Chapter 5—Determining Break-Even Cost. Knowing the break-even cost allows you to draw a line in the sand that you will not cross, and helps you determine the point at which a job will begin to make a profit.

Chapter 6—The Bid Price. Once you know the break-even cost of a job, you need to add profit. This chapter helps you determine the selling price.

Chapter 7—Unit Pricing. Unit pricing is a method that "streamlines" the estimating process by grouping components of the installation together into units. This method has its strengths and shortcomings which we will explain.

Chapter 8—Software-Based Estimating. This chapter will help you understand the technical aspects of computer-assisted estimates. It explains the hardware requirements and the options in selecting software. If you are considering purchasing estimating software in the future, review this chapter to help you with your decision-making process.

Chapter 9—The Bid Process Review. Chapter 9 contains a short overview of the estimating and bids steps that are discussed in Chapters 1 through 6.

Author's Comments

This textbook does not contain any specifics on estimating industrial wiring. However, once you understand the proper technique of estimating, you should have no problem estimating any job with which you have experience. This includes industrial wiring, fire alarms, service stations, hospitals, restaurants, and so on.

There is no glossary of terms because each new term or concept is explained as you proceed.

Difficult Concepts

As you progress through this textbook, you might find you do not understand every explanation, example, calculation, or comment. If you have difficulty with a question or section in the textbook, skip it for the moment and get back to it later. Do not frustrate yourself! The answer key is helpful, so be sure to review the answers to those questions that you miss.

You can also highlight any confusing section of the textbook and discuss the issue with someone who can provide additional insight. If you are still confused, visit www.MikeHolt.com and post your question on the Code Forum for help.

After you have completed this textbook in its entirety, take the time to review those areas you previously had problems with. You might be surprised to see that most of those "sticky points" have been cleared up.

QR Codes

A QR (Quick Reader) Code gives you the ability to use your smartphone to take a "photo" (using a barcode reader app) and be directed to the corresponding website. For example, this QR Code will direct your smartphone to the Mike Holt Enterprises website. To use QR Codes, you'll need an QR app for your smartphone. It might already have the ability to do so, but if not, visit www.mobile-barcodes.com software for more information.

Textbook Errors and Corrections

If you believe there is an error of any kind in this textbook (typographical, grammatical, or technical), no matter how insignificant, please let us know.

Any errors found after printing are listed on our Website, so if you find an error, first check to see if it has already been corrected. Go to www.MikeHolt.com, click on the "Books" link, and then the "Corrections" link (www.MikeHolt.com/bookcorrections.htm). If you do not find the error listed on the website, contact us by e-mailing Corrections@MikeHolt.com. Be sure to include the book title, page number, and any other pertinent information.

YouTube

Visit the Mike Holt channel on YouTube to see video clips that accompany this and other Mike Holt books (www.youtube.com/MikeHoltNEC).

Estimating DVD Program

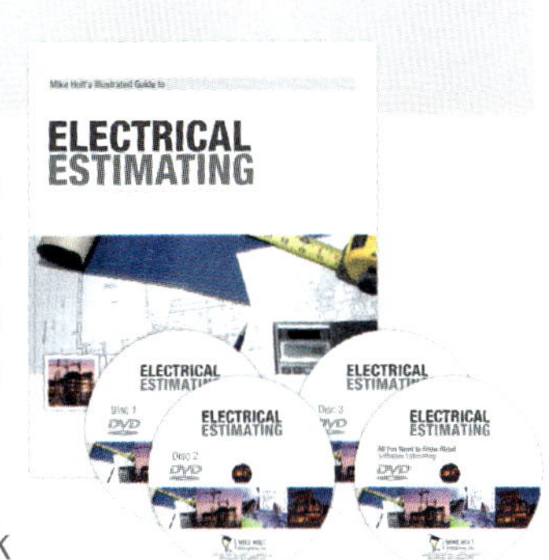

For a more complete understanding of estimating, watch the DVDs that Mike created for this textbook. Mike has brought together project managers, estimators, contractors and an estimating software developer to review the book in a small class format, and bring the material to life.

- DVD 1 and 2: Provide an in-depth analysis of the textbook
- DVD 3: Provides a step-by-step process of how to apply the material
- DVD 4: Explores computer estimating software and its role in your business

Call our office for special pricing on the DVD stand-alone package: 888.632.2633.

About the Author

About the Author

Mike Holt worked his way up through the electrical trade. He began as an apprentice electrician and became one of the most recognized experts in the world as it relates to electrical power installations. He has worked as a journeyman electrician, master electrician, and electrical contractor. Mike's experience in the real world gives him a unique understanding of how the *NEC* relates to electrical installations from a practical standpoint. You'll find his writing style to be clear, concise and easy to understand.

Did you know that he didn't finish high school? So if you struggled in high school or if you didn't finish it at all, don't let this get you down, you're in good company. As a matter of fact, Mike Culbreath, Master Electrician, who produces the finest electrical graphics in the history of the electrical industry, didn't finish high school either. So two high school dropouts produced the text and graphics in this textbook! However, realizing success depends on one's continuing pursuit of education. Mike immediately attained his GED (as did Mike Culbreath) and ultimately attended the University of Miami's Graduate School for a Master's degree in Business Administration (MBA).

Mike Holt resides in Central Florida, is the father of seven children, and has many outside interests and activities. He's a six-time National Barefoot Water-Ski Champion (1988, 1999, 2005, 2006, 2007, and 2008), has set many national records, has competed in three World Championships (2006, 2008, and 2010) and continues to train and work out year-round so that he can qualify to ski in the 2012 World Barefoot Championships at the age of 61!

What sets him apart from some is his commitment to living a balanced lifestyle; placing God first, family, career, then self.

Special Acknowledgments

First, I want to thank God for my godly wife who's always by my side and my children, Belynda, Melissa, Autumn, Steven, Michael, Meghan, and Brittney.

A special thank you must be sent to the staff at the National Fire Protection Association (NFPA), publishers of the *NEC*—in particular Jeff Sargent for his assistance in answering my many *Code* questions over the years. Jeff, you're a "first class" guy, and I admire your dedication and commitment to helping others understand the *NEC*. Other former NFPA staff members I would like to thank include John Caloggero, Joe Ross, and Dick Murray for their help in the past.

A personal thank you goes to Sarina, my long-time friend and office manager. It's been wonderful working side-by-side with you for over 25 years nurturing this company's growth from its small beginnings.

Mike Holt Enterprises Team

Graphic Illustrator

Mike Culbreath devoted his career to the electrical industry and worked his way up from an apprentice electrician to master electrician. While working as a journeyman electrician, he suffered a serious on-the-job knee injury. With a keen interest in continuing education for electricians, he completed courses at Mike Holt Enterprises and then passed the exam to receive his Master Electrician's license. In 1986, after attending classes at Mike Holt Enterprises, he joined the staff to update material and later studied computer graphics and began illustrating Mike Holt's textbooks and magazine articles. He's worked with the company for over 25 years and, as Mike Holt has proudly acknowledged, has helped to transform his words and visions into lifelike graphics.

Editorial and Production Team

I would like to thank Toni Culbreath and Barbara Parks who worked tirelessly to proofread and edit the final stages of this publication. Their attention to detail and dedication to this project is greatly appreciated. I would like to thank Cathleen Kwas who did the layout and production of this book. Her desire to create the best possible product for our customers is appreciated.

Video Team Members

The following special persons provided assistance in the development of this textbook, particularly in ensuring that the technical content is accurate. In addition, they all provided outstanding technical advice as they served on the video team along with author Mike Holt.

Kenneth F. Gordon
Estimator / Project Manager
Terrance Electric & Technology
Bensenville, IL
[DVD 1 and 2]

Ken Gordon has been involved in the electrical construction industry since 1974, starting with a family electrical firm owned primarily by uncles and cousins. First driving material delivery trucks, he was soon introduced to doing take-offs and the estimating process. He then became involved in project management, with a good deal of guidance from cousins Phil and Jim Gordon. Ken passed his Chicago Electrical Contractor's License exam in 1987.

Ken is currently working as an estimator/project manager with Terrance Electric & Technology Co., where he's been since 1998. His duties also include preparing AutoCAD drawings for design/build projects and as-builts. Ken participates in the forums at MikeHolt.com, which he says have been essential to finding *Code* references and solutions to unusual problems.

He developed an interest in teaching when he became a trainer with Trade Service Corporation for their A.L.E.C. Estimating System, travelling nationwide to conduct hands-on training classes for 3 years. He worked as a sales representative and did technical support, on-site training, and system installations for TRF Systems for 7 years. He continues to teach estimating and AutoCAD night classes at the Electric Association of Chicago, where he has been for nearly 15 years.

Ken has been happily married to his wife Maryann for 29 years, and they have four children together: Andy, Amy, Sean, and Megan. An ongoing project has been remodeling their home where they have lived for 25 years, doing much of the work themselves. Other interests include hypermiling (driving for maximum mpg), computer gaming, working on his 1965 Amphicar, and restoring an antique wooden runabout.

Michael Holt, Jr.
Owner
Premier Power, Inc.
Groveland, FL
michael@premierpowerinc.com
www.PremierPowerInc.com
[DVD 3 and 4]

Michael Holt, Jr. is the son of Charles M. Holt (aka Mike Holt) and has been exposed to the electrical trade his whole life. He is a master electrician and Florida Certified Electrical Contractor.

Michael enjoys jet skiing, motocross racing, and stand-up comedy, both as a performer and a member of the audience. He is very much a "people person" and very active socially.

Michael has a daughter, Haylee, whom he absolutely adores.

Daniel Brian House
Dan House Electric, Inc
Ocala, FL
www.DanHouseElectric.com
[DVD 3 and 4]

Brian House is a high-energy entrepreneur with a passion for doing business the right way. Brian is currently the CEO of Dan House Electric, Inc., an unlimited electrical contracting company based in Florida and working throughout the SE United States.

He's been involved in varying aspects of alternative energy and energy conservation since the 1990s and has a passion for constantly improving the combinations of technology offered to his customers, whether designing energy-efficient lighting retrofits, exploring "green" biomass generators, or partnering with solar energy companies as their preferred installer. Brian has experienced the laughs and tears of "the growing up of" alternative energy and looks to the future for more exciting developments.

Currently, he is preparing for his NABCEP certification and exploring the future of cutting edge "green" technologies with a new start-up company. In addition to managing his growing company, Brian also speaks at various training and motivational seminars and classes. Passionate about helping others, he regularly engages with the youth of the local community to motivate them into exploring their future.

Brian and his wife Carissa have shared the joy of their four children and over 30 foster children during a happy 13 years of marriage. When not at work or church, he's an avid fly fisherman preferring the action-packed intercoastals for his angling venue.

Thomas Landa
Project Manager / Estimator
Shelby Township, MI
TNT8197@Yahoo.com
[DVD 1 and 2]

Tom Landa is a Project Manager/Estimator and has been involved in the electrical industry for the better part of 30 years. He worked his way up through the electrical field, starting as an apprentice at an early age, following his family's preceding path. Tom has been intrigued in this ever-changing business since day one and he's continually striving to be the best at what he can do. Electricity and this business are his life and he feels that he's been educated from an early age to provide a quality end result for his customers, family, friends, and everyone he's had the benefit of coming into contact with in this industry. Tom feels that this can be accomplished through dedication to your trade, along with a strong education base, honesty, and integrity.

Tom continues to put forth everything he has every day of every week for his beautiful wife TinaAnne and their two amazing sons (Tommaso and Antonio) she and God have allowed him the luxury of having. Without the aforementioned, he could not be where he is in life today.

Gary L. Newton
Project Manager / Chief Estimator
Consulting Electrical Engineers
Sacramento, CA
[DVD 1 and 2]

Gary Newton entered the U.S. Army after completing high school. His time in the service of his country included a tour in Vietnam as a Combat Engineer. After the Army, Gary worked for telephone and cable TV companies. He completed an apprenticeship as a land surveyor, then a stint in the San Diego shipyards as a journeyman maintenance electrician. Gary spent 3 more years as a small, independent Electrical Contractor and estimator.

In 1980, he went to work as an electrical designer for a local consulting engineering company. Since then, Gary has worked for consulting engineering companies in California, Nevada, and Colorado. Projects have included commercial, industrial, institutional, governmental, and public agencies. The past 7 years have been mostly school design for the State of California.

Gary has worked on over 1,000 projects with development of over 18 million sq ft of space. His completed projects include: overhead and underground distribution systems (including sub-stations), building lighting and power layouts, telecom and data centers, large scale communication backbone systems, UPS and power conditioning projects, power generation with multiple generators and paralleling switchgear, special engineering projects, and graphics applications. Cost estimates have been an integral part of all projects; working with established budgets, setting construction budgets, or responding to change order and value engineering requests. In 1987, Gary was awarded the Certified Professional Estimator certificate by the American Society of Professional Estimators.

He presently lives in Sacramento, CA, with his wife of 31 years, his two grown children, and a grandson. Gary has an older daughter living in San Diego, who has his other three grandsons.

Bill Ruffner
Founder and CEO
TurboBid
Chicago, IL
www.TurboBid.net
[DVD 3 and 4]

Bill Ruffner is the founder and CEO of the award-winning TurboBid estimating software program. It was introduced to the marketplace in 2006 and has become one of the leading estimating software programs in the industry. TurboBid is designed to help contractors win more profitable business by providing a systematic process to identify all costs, maximize crew productivity, and present a professional image.

In 1991, Bill started working as an apprentice for one of Chicagoland's largest electrical contractors. During a 10 year period, hard work and dedication allowed him to quickly advance through the company. In 1997, Bill was offered and accepted the position of Vice President. During his four years in that position, he was responsible for increasing the company's annual revenue from eight million dollars to over twenty two million dollars a year.

In 2001, he started his own electrical contracting company. Bill knew that the company's success would ultimately depend on his ability to quickly generate accurate estimates. He also understood that his customers would form an initial opinion of his company based on the quality and professional appearance of the proposals and bid package documents he presented to them. Bill believed that the fastest and most accurate method to estimate electrical jobs was undoubtedly with the use of a computer. Unfortunately, he couldn't find an estimating program that met his requirements. The available programs were either far too complicated, didn't generate a quality bid package, or were much too expensive. "That's when I decided to take matters into my own hands," says Ruffner. "The only way that I was going to get an estimating program that met all of my needs was if I created one myself." Enter TurboBid.

In 2003, Bill hired the best software programmer in the industry to help take his estimating program from the design stage into a fully functioning software program. While he used his 20+ years of experience as an electrician and contractor to design the software, his skilled programming team brought the software to life in a powerful yet easy to use format. The end result was simply amazing. It quickly became one of the best-selling estimating programs available at any price.

Currently, whenever Bill isn't busy conducting live on-line training classes with TurboBid users, he continues to design and add amazing new features to the program. He enjoys spending any free time that he may have with his beautiful wife of over 20 years. His son is currently enrolled in Arizona State University's (ASU) School of Business with plans of joining the company upon graduation.

Perry D. Vogler
Done Right Electric, Inc.
Wildwood, FL
donerightelect@aol.com
www.solar-dr.com
[DVD 1 and 2]

Perry Vogler is a State certified Master Electrician in Florida, Georgia, Alabama, North Carolina, and Missouri, and is NABCEP solar certified.

He and his family moved to Central Florida in 2001 and started Done Right Electric shortly after that. They work on custom residential and small to mid-size commercial jobs, design/build and electrical engineering, and also specialize in solar power and building efficiency. Perry has spent his entire life in the electrical and building trades, learning work in all trades so he can incorporate this with building efficiency. This often gives him the edge he needs to win the job, and expand the work he does for his customers.

Perry is happily married and has two boys. He is currently training his oldest to be an electrician and a solar installer. His hobbies are solar and building efficiency as well as playing and coaching fast-pitch softball, playing guitar, and studying electric and solar power.

James Wescott
Electrical Contractor
Aston, PA
[DVD 1 and 2]

Jim Wescott, after serving for 4 years in Germany (1960 through 1964) with the Signal Corps, returned home and worked in the family business for 2 years as an electrician doing commercial and industrial electrical work. From 1966 to 1978, he worked for four large electrical contractors in Philadelphia learning estimating and project management skills by day and attending school for Business Administration at night. Jim attained his Associates degree in Business Administration in 1974.

In 1978, he formed a partnership with his father and a brother. While they continued doing commercial and industrial work, they decided to turn their greater efforts to the Public Works market, which is their niche today. They currently have about 50 employees and work in Pennsylvania, New Jersey, Delaware, and Maryland.

Jim learned estimating at a NECA estimating course in 1967. In 1978, he and his family purchased the first desktop Electrical Estimating program on the market developed by Trade Service, which ran on a Radio Shack Model II desktop computer. James taught an estimating course for the Southeast Pennsylvania Chapter of the Associated Builders and Contractors.

The first lesson he learned from a trade organization at the age of 15 was that, "your best friends in the construction industry are your competitors." That experience prompted him to live with the philosophy that the more you help your peers, the better the industry, and the more you educate the competition, the more competitive you become. James has a strong desire to help educate young contractors so they can be legitimate, successful competitors. An ignorant, uneducated competitor is our worst enemy.

INTRODUCTION

INTRODUCTION

This chapter lays the foundation for your increased understanding of the process of electrical estimating and submitting bids. It also covers the basic concepts about estimating and bidding that all electrical contractors must understand in order to be successful in business.

A large percentage of electrical firms obtain most of their electrical construction and maintenance work through this process, and the bid price must be based on a solid estimate. A correct estimate determines what it will cost you to complete the job according to the customer's needs, as described in the drawings and specifications.

The "lowest" price and the "best" price are not necessarily the same thing. The failure to understand this is perhaps the major reason why so many electrical firms go out of business each year. If you now understand this one concept, this course has already paid for itself. As you continue forward, you will gain even more insight and value. What you learn about estimating will help your business be successful and it will help you personally.

Electrical contractors are awarded most of their work through either competitive or negotiated bidding. The bid price must be acceptable to your customer and include sufficient profit for your firm to stay in business.

CAUTION: *If it is discovered after the bid has been submitted that you made an error, the customer might accept an amended bid, reject the bid outright, or hold you to your price as per the submitted bid. Even though there might be penalties having to do with a bid bond and/or your reputation, it is important to communicate with the customer, especially if the error represents a significant cost. Of course, if this happens too often your credibility will begin to decrease.*

Competitive Bids

Competitive bid work requires the contractor to submit a price or a set of prices the company will charge to perform the services required in accordance with the drawings and specifications. This bid process requires competing contractors to submit bids and the customer chooses from among them.

Author's Comment: Customers often look at more than just the bid price; factors that might be considered include a previous relationship, satisfaction with previous work, the contractor's attitude, the firm's reputation and its experience relating to the work to be done, the technical approach of how the specified work will be

Notes

completed in the time required, and whether the company has adequate resources to complete the project in a timely manner. Many contractors like this type of bidding because everything is laid out so everyone is bidding on the "same page." Efficiency and organization on the jobsite ultimately determine profitability.

Negotiated Bids

Negotiated bid work usually does not require competitive bidding; instead, the electrical contractor deals directly with the customer—perhaps a general contractor or owner for whom the contractor has worked in the past. Together, they negotiate a price based on what the customer needs.

If you enter a negotiation knowing how much it will cost you for the project (estimate), then you will be able to negotiate the job price and schedule from a position of knowledge. Not only will you have more power in the negotiations, but those you are negotiating with will have more confidence with your price.

CAUTION: *Going into a negotiation without an estimate means you will negotiate without knowing how or what you agree to will affect your schedule or budget. You can easily end up agreeing to things you will not be able to deliver, possibly at a cost that is above what you anticipated. Things may sound doable at the time, but once you "work up the numbers" or review other information a good estimate contains, you may discover that you have just set your firm up for cascading cash-flow problems, resource conflicts, or even failure to perform. A good estimating system reduces the likelihood of creating these problems.*

Best Value Bids

This type of bid is similar to negotiated bidding and is used when working with an owner or general contractor.

1.1 Estimating versus Bidding

Determining the selling price for a job has two separate components, the estimate price and the bid price. The estimate total is what the job will cost you to complete. Profit is then added and the new total is the bid price which is the amount you wish the customer to agree to pay for the work performed.

Notes

The Estimate Price

The purpose of estimating is to determine the cost of a project before you actually do the work. Estimating must take into consideration variable job conditions, the cost of materials, labor cost, labor availability, direct job expenses, and management costs (overhead).

The Bid Price

Once you know the estimated cost of a project (your cost), you add profit to determine the selling (bid) price of the job. Methods and formulas for the addition of profit will be covered later in this textbook.

1.2 A Good Estimating System

A good estimating system should help you to quickly and accurately determine the cost of a project in a manner that includes all anticipated costs. To be efficient and accurate, it must be systematic and routine in order to keep errors to a minimum.

1.3 Objectives and Purpose of an Electrical Contractor

All businesses exist for one reason and that is to make money (profit)! So while you may enjoy your work (and I hope you do) or are even passionate about it (and I hope you are), the purpose of an electrical contractor is to make a profit on every single job. Profit is a reward for taking risks, so it is important to be aware of and evaluate the degree of risk contained in each job. Providing the best service, with the most profit possible considering the market, is essential to your success.

To be a successful electrical contractor, you must provide a quality service to your customers at a competitive price where the price is greater than your actual cost. Successful electrical contracting is really just that simple—providing a quality electrical installation at a competitive price that exceeds your actual cost. Therefore, the first step to becoming a successful electrical contractor is to determine your expected cost.

1.4 Why So Many Electrical Contractors Are Unsuccessful

Most electrical contractors wear many hats—estimator, project manager, secretary, warehouse person, truck driver, supervisor, electrician, salesperson, and so on. There are not enough hours in the day or night to keep up with all of the demands of running a successful

Notes

contracting business. If an electrical contractor is not careful, he or she might forget the most important hat—managing the job to ensure that a profit is made.

There are many reasons why people lose money on jobs:

- Forgetting to include costs, thinking there is no overhead because you are working out of your house
- Being too trusting and finding the customer cannot pay
- Missing things on the bid
- Forgetting to bill things out (including the job itself)
- Not following up to ensure payment is received (not paying attention to detail)
- Not seeking help before getting into trouble

Remember to manage the job to ensure that a profit is ALWAYS made on EVERY job! You must make that firm commitment.

If you do not know how to properly determine the cost of a job (estimate), you are not likely to be in business very long. Failure to know the cost of doing business (estimating) is probably the number one reason contractors fail. If your bids are high (too much profit), you will not get much work. If your bids are low (no profit), you will get lots of work, but of course you will have to close up shop.

Successful contractors manage projects to ensure profit. The estimate becomes your budget and you must track that job to be sure the targeted amount of profit is met. Actual cost is affected by job management. Estimating is both a science (gathering costs) and an art form (effectively managing the job).

With over 75,000 electrical contractors in the United States, competition is fierce. The successful electrical contractor must manage projects so he or she can compete profitably in today's highly competitive marketplace. The actual cost of any project is significantly affected by how well the job is managed.

1.5 Project Management

To properly manage a job, the project manager must have a budget, and the budget is derived from the estimate. The job budget must describe what material is required for each phase of the job, and when it will be needed. It must also describe the types and amount of labor (the number of hours, and the number and type of electricians) required to complete each phase of the job, and as with material, when it will be needed. With proper information, the project manager will be better prepared to complete the project as planned, and ensure it comes in at (or under) budget and a profit is made.

Notes

Author's Comment: Information for project management is easy to acquire using computer-assisted estimating software.

Proper project management makes the difference between profit and loss on a properly estimated project. Effective job planning, labor scheduling, and material purchasing are all factors in the ultimate cost of a project. The field manager must understand how the job was estimated and continuous communication between the electricians performing the work in the field, the project manager, and the estimator is essential for profit.

Without a proper job budget, you will not know what materials or tools you need or when you need them. This can, and often does, result in not having the material or the tools on the job in a timely manner (poor field performance). That situation means your workers stand around wasting time and money. If you fail to manage your material properly, you might have too much on the job, thereby increasing the likelihood of it being damaged, wasted, stolen, or incurring unanticipated costs for moving extra material around the jobsite (handling multiple times).

Job management requires the project manager to know what labor is needed and when. Insufficient manpower can create conflicts with the other trades and with the owner. Too much manpower on the job at the wrong time results in lower productivity and increased costs that cannot be recovered. If you are going to be successful as an electrical contractor, you must manage your material and labor so they are at the job when required thereby ensuring productivity in accordance with the estimate and job schedule. You must also manage them in accordance with the estimate and agreed upon schedule.

As a job progresses it is often necessary to adjust the budget (estimate) based on information and feedback from the jobsite. Job conditions might be different than those expected, or the project manager, field manager, and/or field personnel might come up with ideas that improve production.

1.6 Can I Be Competitive?

A collapsing market may make it difficult to win jobs because of the increase in competition. You might try focusing on your area of expertise rather than bidding on jobs with which you have no experience.

Most electrical contractors are concerned about their ability to be competitive, make money, and stay in business. To be competitive and profitable, he or she must offer the customer a quality service at a reasonable price. To accomplish this, the electrical contractor must control the job and administrative (overhead) costs so they are within the estimated budget. Factors that affect a contractor's competitiveness include:

Notes

- Competition
- Cost of Material (Buying Power)
- Experience
- Labor Cost and Productivity
- Management Skills
- Overhead
- Selling the Job at Your Price

Competition

Make it a point to know who your competitors are, and what their capabilities are. Look at their Website, and visit jobs they have done so you can see their quality of workmanship and areas of specialization. Talk to your crews in the field, as they are often a gold mine for this type of information.

Consider the number of contractors bidding the job. When possible, try not to bid jobs that have more than four competitors. This is because the greater the number of competitors, the greater the chance that someone will make a mistake and have a "low-ball" price. On the other hand, if there are fewer than three competitors, you can probably raise your profit margin and still be competitive. Be knowledgeable about your competitions' capacity and their work on hand relative to that capacity.

Small contractors cannot be as price-competitive as larger contractors because the overhead for smaller contractors is higher (as a percentage) in relationship to material and labor costs and they are not able to purchase material at the same level of discount pricing that large contractors can receive. Small contractors often have poor management skills, but might have better focus and service. Fortunately for the smaller contractor, larger contractors do not always fish in the same pond, nor do they typically offer the personal service that some customers demand.

Cost of Material

Suppliers seldom acknowledge it, but they offer different prices to different contractors for the same material. What can you do to be offered the best price? Start by becoming a good customer and making it in the suppliers' best interest to give you the best price. A few simple rules for receiving the best price are to shop around and check prices. Also, pay your bills on time so you can take advantage of any discounts offered. Some suppliers will give their best paying contractors lower prices during the estimating period.

Did you know that it costs more to pick your material up at the supply house counter than it does to have it delivered? Do not pick up your material if you have the option of having it delivered. You should check with the supplier to be sure that the cost will be the same, but realize that you have to cover the cost of your labor if you pick up material as opposed to having it delivered.

Some contractors buy commonly used commodity items in large quantities to obtain a lower price which they can use in their estimate. They weigh the cost of financing, storage, and double handling against their price advantage.

Author's Comment: The lowest price is not everything; you will want a relationship with a supplier who will help you solve your problems and who will be there when needed. Always remember the big picture (just like you want your customers to do).

Notes

Experience

The more experience you and your employees have with a given type of construction, the fewer mistakes will be made and the more efficient and productive the job will be. This means you will be able to do the job with less labor time, resulting in a reduction in the estimated cost. Each job carries a degree of risk which can be affected by the amount of experience you have with that type of job.

To be competitive in a market you are not familiar with, you need to educate yourself by attending seminars, reading trade magazines, and watching training DVDs. Do whatever you can to minimize your inexperience. But the labor cost for the first job in a new market will always be higher than following jobs.

Another factor that must be considered when determining the bid price of an unfamiliar type of work is risk, particularly the risk that labor will be higher than you estimated. The greater the perceived risk, the higher the profit margin needs to be in order to offset possible losses. If you bid work with which you are experienced, your profit margin can be higher and your bid can still be competitive.

When you have submitted a bid and you are not awarded the job, ask the customer for a briefing to review your costs and technical approach. This will help build valuable estimating knowledge for a particular type of project and customer to help you be more competitive on future bids.

Notes

Labor Cost and Productivity

Competitiveness between contractors based on different pay scales can be significant; some pay rock-bottom wages and others pay union scale. You need to pay your electricians a competitive salary and provide suitable benefits to discourage them from leaving for greener pastures. The salary should compensate them for their abilities and their contribution to your company's bottom line. By paying top dollar with benefits, you should be able to hire and retain highly skilled, motivated, educated electricians to work for you for years, if not a lifetime.

It is not necessary to pay all electricians the same wage; higher skilled electricians earn the company more and should be paid more. They also motivate the lesser skilled to become more skilled.

Having motivated, loyal, and skilled electricians who have been with your organization for years will ultimately result in a lower labor installation cost as opposed to having an unhappy and unskilled labor force who feel no loyalty to your company. If you pay low wages, you can expect problems with your employees, the inspector, general contractors, and other trades. This all spills over into the customer's experience with your company. Remember these are the persons that represent your company and interface directly with your customers.

Management Skills

Successful electrical contractors know how to manage their labor and material in accordance with the estimate. Failure to manage the project in accordance with the estimate means that it is unlikely you will make the profit you projected. Many electrical contractors are electricians without formal business management training; as a result, they do not do a very good job as a business owner. They often prefer to "work with the tools" rather than "deal with the paper work" of the business. But if you want to be a successful electrical contractor, then you need to attend management seminars, watch training DVDs, and become involved with a local contractors' organization.

Many electrical contractors do not realize that they are not alone in their experiences. By joining an electrical contractors' organization you will gain the experience of those who have been there before you. Learning from another contractor's misfortune is always better than making the mistake yourself. In the construction industry it is a fact that your best friends are your competitors. An uneducated, unethical contractor is the biggest hindrance to obtaining a fair price for your work. In many parts of the country there are local electrical contractors' organizations that many contractors join.

In addition, there are two well-respected national electrical contractor associations:

Notes

Independent Electrical Contractors, Inc. (IEC)
4401 Ford Avenue, Suite 1100
Alexandria, VA 22302
Telephone: 800.456.4324, or 703.549.7351
Fax: 703.549.7448
www.ieci.org

National Electrical Contractors Association (NECA)
3 Bethesda Metro Center, Suite 1100
Bethesda, MD 20814-5372
Telephone: 301.657.3110
Fax: 301.215.4500
www.necanet.org

Overhead

Overhead expenses are those costs that are required to operate the business such as telephones, shop rent, vehicles, advertising, insurance, office personnel, and so on. Since overhead costs represent between 20 and 40 percent of an electrical contractor's total sales, it is critical to keep that cost as low as possible.

Selling the Job at Your Price

Confidence and professionalism are important ingredients in getting your price. Confidence comes from knowing your price is a good value to the customer and that they will be pleased with the quality of service you provide. Next to confidence is professionalism. Do you come across as a professional by your appearance and the appearance of your workers and vehicles? Many electrical contractors dress and carry themselves as a tradesman rather than a business person. When you are meeting with the customer, dress as a business person. But it does not stop there; ensure that your electricians and vehicles have a professional appearance. If you provide outstanding service at a reasonable price, then you will "close" more contracts if you come across as a professional business organization.

What do the customers want? Do they want a quality installation at a fair price, or are they willing to accept an inferior job as long as the price is low? Price is a major factor, but it is not the only factor - low price, without quality service often results in an unhappy customer. With proper management you can provide a quality installation and in the long run a quality installation at a fair price will be more cost-effective for your customers and better for your reputation.

Notes

1.7 The Electrical Market

Many contractors develop a niche (a special place) in the market such as service, housing, medical facilities, banking, commercial buildings, or industrial maintenance.

> **CAUTION:** *The electrical industry is in constant change—parts of the market are expanding or contracting depending on technology, the economy, and customers' needs. So be careful, do not put all of your eggs in one basket or you might find your niche almost disappearing, as happened when the housing market collapsed in 2007.*

New and expanding markets offer greater opportunities to develop new customers, possibly with fewer competitors and greater profit margins. Consider every bid request as an opportunity to monitor the market's direction, and then decide which path you will choose to follow.

1.8 Negotiated Work

Some electrical contractors, based on past performance (honesty, quality service, and professionalism), have a secure long-term relationship with the customer where they have the opportunity to negotiate the price of an upcoming project. This is a fragile but lucrative market that can be maintained only when the electrical contractor is honest in pricing and provides outstanding service that meets or exceeds the customer's expectations. Maintaining these kinds of clients requires a higher level of record keeping and client interaction.

1.9 Best Value

This type of bid is similar to negotiated bidding and is used when working with an owner or general contractor. Your goal is to show the value being brought to your customer to support the bid submitted. Compromise on the bid price can be reached (for example) by suggesting less expensive material than shown on the plans and specifications that will still meet the customer's needs.

CHAPTER 1

Summary

Notes

Introduction

A large percentage of electrical firms obtain most of their electrical construction and maintenance work through the process of estimating and submitting bids, and the price must be based on a solid estimate. A correct estimate determines what it will cost you to complete the job according to the customer's needs, as described in the drawings and specifications. Electrical contractors are awarded most of their work through either competitive or negotiated bidding.

1.1 Estimating versus Bidding

Determining the selling price for a job has two separate components, the estimate price and the bid price.

1.2 A Good Estimating System

A good estimating system should help you to quickly and accurately determine the cost of a project in a manner that includes all anticipated costs. To be efficient and accurate, it must be systematic and routine in order to keep errors to a minimum.

1.3 Objectives and Purpose of an Electrical Contractor

The purpose of an electrical contractor is to make a profit on every single job. To be a successful electrical contractor, you must provide a quality service to your customers at a competitive price where the price is greater than your actual cost.

1.4 Why So Many Electrical Contractors are Unsuccessful

If you do not know how to properly determine the cost of a job (estimate), you are not likely to be in business very long. Failure to know the cost of doing business (estimating) is probably the number one reason contractors fail. If your bids are high (too much profit), you will not get much work. If your bids are low (no profit), you will get lots of work, but of course you will have to close up shop.

The successful electrical contractor must manage projects so he or she can compete profitably in today's highly competitive marketplace. The actual cost of any project is significantly affected by how well the job is managed.

Notes

To properly manage a job, the project manager must have a budget, and the budget is derived from the estimate. It must describe what material is required, when material is needed, and the types and amount of labor required to complete each phase of the job.

1.5 Project Management

Proper project management makes the difference between profit and loss on a project. Effective job planning, labor scheduling, and material purchasing are all factors in the ultimate cost of a project. The field manager must understand how the job was estimated.

1.6 Can I Be Competitive?

Most electrical contractors are concerned about their ability to be competitive, make money, and stay in business. Factors that affect a contractor's competitiveness include:

- Competition
- Cost of Material (Buying Power)
- Experience
- Labor Cost and Productivity
- Management Skills
- Overhead
- Selling the Job at Your Price

1.7 The Electrical Market

Many contractors develop a niche (a special place) in the market such as service, housing, medical facilities, banking, commercial buildings, or industrial maintenance.

New and expanding markets offer greater opportunities to develop new customers, possibly with fewer competitors and greater profit margins. Consider every bid request as an opportunity to monitor the market's direction, and then decide which path you will choose to follow.

1.8 Negotiated Work

Some electrical contractors, based on past performance (honesty, quality service, and professionalism), have a secure long-term relationship with the customer where they have the opportunity to negotiate the price of an upcoming project. This is a fragile but lucrative market that can be maintained only when the electrical contractor is honest in pricing and provides outstanding service that meets or exceeds the customer's expectations.

1.9 Best Value

Notes

This type of bid is similar to negotiated bidding and is used when working with an owner or general contractor. Your goal is to show the value being brought to your customer to support the bid submitted.

CHAPTER
1

Conclusion

Notes

One of the most important things you have learned in this chapter is the purpose of electrical contracting. It is a business… and businesses exist to make money! That does not mean charging the most you can get by with or cheating customers, because companies that do such things tend not to be around for very long.

It means charging the correct prices and doing the work the right way so you can justify those prices. Many electrical contractors are unsuccessful because their prices are wrong. The solution is not merely to raise prices or to lower them. You have to charge the "right" price, and to do that you need to know what it costs to do a given job—that is where estimating comes in.

A good estimate is the foundation for a good bid and the budget needed to properly manage the job.

Essay Questions

Notes

1. How do electrical contractors obtain most of their work?

2. What are the two components used to determine the selling price for a job?

3. What are three important qualities of a good estimating system?

4. How can you be a successful electrical contractor?

5. Why are many electrical contractors unsuccessful?

6. What information is derived from the estimate for the budget the project manager must have in order to properly manage a job?

Notes

7. What factors affect a contractor's ability to be competitive?

8. Identify some of the markets in which a contractor might develop a niche.

9. What is negotiated work?

10. What is best value work?

Multiple-Choice Questions

Notes

Introduction

1. Competitive bid work requires the contractor to submit a price or a set of prices the company will charge to perform the services required in accordance with the ______.

   (a) drawings
   (b) specifications
   (c) a or b
   (d) a and b

2. Negotiated bid work usually does not require competitive bidding; instead, the electrical contractor deals directly with the ______.

   (a) customer
   (b) inspector
   (c) other trades
   (d) none of these

1.1 Estimating versus Bidding

3. The purpose of ______ is to determine the cost of a project before you actually do the work.

   (a) negotiating
   (b) bidding
   (c) estimating
   (d) selling

4. Estimating must take into consideration ______, the cost of materials, labor cost, labor availability, direct job expenses, and management costs (overhead).

   (a) the inspector
   (b) variable job conditions
   (c) weather conditions
   (d) all of these

Notes

5. Once you know the estimated cost of a project, you add ______ to determine the selling (bid) price of the job.

   (a) overhead
   (b) profit
   (c) labor burden
   (d) none of these

1.2 A Good Estimating System

6. To be efficient and accurate, a good estimating system must be systematic and routine in order to keep ______ to a minimum.

   (a) errors
   (b) profit
   (c) cost
   (d) overhead

1.3 Objectives and Purpose of an Electrical Contractor

7. The purpose of an electrical contractor is to ______.

   (a) stay in business
   (b) determine the cost of every job offered
   (c) treat employees fairly
   (d) make a profit on every single job

8. The first step to becoming a successful electrical contractor is to determine your ______.

   (a) overhead
   (b) expected cost
   (c) profit margin
   (d) labor burden

1.4 Why So Many Electrical Contractors are Unsuccessful

Notes

9. Failure to know the ______ is probably the number one reason contractors fail.

(a) *National Electrical Code*
(b) market
(c) cost of doing business (estimating)
(d) all of these

10. The actual cost of any project is significantly affected by how well ______.

(a) the job is managed
(b) overhead is applied
(c) market changes are anticipated
(d) the general contractor maintains the schedule

1.5 Project Management

11. The factor(s) pertaining to the ultimate cost of a project is(are) ______.

(a) effective job planning
(b) labor scheduling
(c) material purchasing
(d) all of these

12. If you are going to be successful as an electrical contractor, you must manage your ______ to ensure that it(they) is(are) at the job when required.

(a) material
(b) labor
(c) a and b
(d) none of these

1.6 Can I Be Competitive?

13. Make it a point to know who your competitors are, and what their ______.

(a) overhead is
(b) capabilities are
(c) profit margin is
(d) expenses are

Notes

14. When possible, try not to bid jobs that have more than ______ competitors.

(a) four
(b) five
(c) six
(d) seven

15. Suppliers seldom acknowledge it, but they offer different prices to different contractors for the same material.

(a) True
(b) False

16. To be competitive in a market you are not familiar with, you need to educate yourself by ______.

(a) attending seminars
(b) reading trade magazines
(c) watching training DVDs
(d) all of these

17. You need to pay your electricians a competitive salary and provide suitable benefits to discourage them from ______.

(a) wasting material
(b) leaving for greener pastures
(c) discussing their wages
(d) being unproductive

18. Most electrical contractors are electricians without formal ______.

(a) electrical management skills
(b) accounting training
(c) business management training
(d) labor management skills

Notes

19. Overhead costs represent between ______ percent of an electrical contractor's total sales.

    (a) 10 and 15
    (b) 15 and 20
    (c) 20 and 30
    (d) 20 and 40

20. ______ is(are) an important ingredient(s) in having your price accepted.

    (a) Professionalism
    (b) Confidence
    (c) a or b
    (d) a and b

1.7 The Electrical Market

21. Consider every ______ as an opportunity to monitor the market's direction, and then decide which path you will choose to follow.

    (a) bid request
    (b) telephone call
    (c) completed estimate
    (d) all of these

1.8 Negotiated Work

22. Some electrical contractors, based on past performance (honesty, quality service, and professionalism), have a secure short-term relationship with the customer where they have the opportunity to negotiate the price of an upcoming project.

    (a) True
    (b) False

Notes

1.9 Best Value

23. Best value bids are similar to ______ bids and are used when working with an owner or general contractor. Your goal is to show the value being brought to your customer to support the bid submitted.

(a) competitive
(b) square foot
(c) negotiated
(d) all of these

CHAPTER

2 ABOUT ESTIMATING

INTRODUCTION

Now that you understand the important role that estimating plays in the electrical industry (and in your company), you are ready to learn more about the process. You also need to understand the responsibilities of an estimator and what resources are needed to meet those responsibilities.

This chapter covers a few other important points about the estimating process, but the most important item you will learn is the "detailed estimating method." With this chapter, you will begin viewing the estimating process as a way of breaking the job down into its individual parts and determining the cost of each.

2.1 Qualities of a Good Estimator

The following is a list of qualities that identify a good estimator:

- A positive mental attitude
- Computer literacy
- A willingness to learn from one's mistakes
- Familiarity with new products and installation methods
- An understanding of construction and the ability to visualize the electrical requirements
- An orderly mind with a tendency to be careful, accurate, and neat
- Decisiveness and the ability to make decisions without being intimidated by details
- Fairness, honesty, and integrity
- Knowledge of the *National Electrical Code* and local electrical codes
- Patience to finish the estimate without frustration
- Organization
- A willingness to stick to and get the job done by putting in whatever time is necessary to meet the bid date and time deadlines

Notes

2.2 Duties and Responsibilities of the Estimator

To prepare an estimate properly, you must have the ability to mentally visualize the material items required and how they are installed to complete the job. While it is "possible" to accurately estimate a job without electrical experience, it is unlikely anyone can do this for anything but the simplest of jobs. Even then it will only be a matter of time before an estimate is terribly wrong. Because electrical work is complex, the estimator needs to have electrical construction experience (preferably as an electrician).

He or she must be able to envision the need for special equipment and/or services that will be required, such as scaffolding, man lifts, cranes, trenching, rigging services, and so on, and include them in the estimate.

Not only do you need to know what is required to complete the job, you must be comfortable with numbers and math as they pertain to *NEC* electrical construction and design calculations. Besides determining the cost of the job, the electrical estimator is often responsible for material purchases and project management information and tracking.

Purchasing Material

The estimator is familiar with the job, so he or she is often expected to order the material required to do the job and to have good negotiating skills with suppliers to arrive at a competitive price.

Computer-Assisted Estimates. A computer-assisted estimate can easily and quickly provide the material items and quantities needed for this purpose.

Project Management/Tracking

The estimator needs to develop the information for the project manager so that he or she can manage the material and labor efficiently and effectively. This information is also essential for job costing. There are many computer programs that are designed to help with the project management task if the estimator is willing to take the time to enter the data and keep it current.

Computer-Assisted Estimates. A computer-assisted estimate will allow you to organize the scope of your work by providing information about what is needed for each phase of the job.

Notes

2.3 The Estimating Workspace and Tools

The Workspace

Before you even think of estimating a job, you need to have the proper workspace and tools. Appropriate lighting is essential. The workspace must be laid out efficiently and be located where the estimator will not be disturbed. It needs to be of adequate size, not just a closet with a desk. Many business managers try to save money in this regard, only to lower the productivity of the estimators and thereby raise the cost of doing business. The workspace should be designed so that everything is within reach from the sitting position, including books, paperwork, telephone, fax machine, computer, and so forth.

Estimating Tools

We all know that performing a job without the proper tools often gives poor results, causes frustration, and takes longer than necessary. Proper estimating tools reduce human errors, increase efficiency, and quickly pay for themselves. The estimator should have the following tools in proper condition:

Adding Machine. Get a large adding machine with paper and large keys.

Aspirin. You will need them.

Bookcases. Bookcases are a must to hold reference materials such as catalogs, literature, and manuals from manufacturers and electrical distributors, and a rack or two for DVDs and CDs.

Calculator. Get a solar-powered calculator so you do not have to worry about batteries and make sure it has a large display with large keys.

Chair. Many estimators prefer to work with an adjustable height swivel chair between two large tables, or between a table and a desk to permit the most efficient use of the workspace. A comfortable chair that rolls and has armrests is a requirement, so do not try to save any money here—a properly fitted chair will pay for itself many times over.

Colored Pencils, Pens, or Highlighters. You will need colored pencils, pens, or fine- and large-tip highlighters to mark symbols on any printouts of the drawings.

Computer. Be sure you have adequate computer resources including spreadsheet and word processing programs. Internet access is necessary to save time in looking up information, contacting customers and suppliers, and doing needed research. An e-mail account is required, not optional, and make sure you have one that contains your company name, rather than using a consumer-grade e-mail service like Hotmail.

Notes

Copy Machine. A copy machine is always needed, but you can purchase a machine that makes copies, scans, and sends and receives faxes. Consider a scanner with an ADF (automatic document feeder) so multiple pages can be easily scanned.

Counter. There are two types of counters—the mechanical type and the electronic type. The mechanical type is designed for use with your left hand. You put your finger through the hole, wrap your hand around it, and press the counter with your left thumb. The electronic counter is designed to be used with either hand and can interface with your estimating software for instant data input.

Desk. A large desk is necessary so you have an adequate work area for paperwork, pencils, pens, mouse, keyboard, and everything else that seems to accumulate. A small work area will force you to continuously struggle to keep things organized and will waste your valuable time.

Digital Plan Wheel and Counter. A digital drawing wheel is used to measure circuit run lengths and has an electronic counter. A built-in digital drawing wheel has the ability to change the scale quickly and is very easy to read and use. These devices also contain a counter feature and can interface with your estimating software.

Draftsman's Measuring Tape. A measuring tape that has a ⅛ in. and a ¼ in. scale.

Filing Cabinets. While it is easier to find things that have been converted from paper to a searchable format, it also takes time to scan things. In many cases, it is still more efficient to keep the paper in filing cabinets.

Lighting. Get plenty of light for the work surface area; a nice desk lamp is never a bad idea.

Magnifying Glass. Some details on the drawings might be difficult to decipher without a magnifying glass. A pair of reading glasses might achieve the same effect hands-free.

Mechanical Pencils. Use a good mechanical pencil with 0.07 lead and an eraser.

Pencil Sharpener. If you use wooden pencils, have an electric pencil sharpener. A battery-powered one will be sufficient if you are not estimating full time; if you are, then get one that operates at 120V.

Personal Stereo with Headphones. Headphones with music can help some people focus as they spend hours and hours estimating.

Plan Table. Since you are often required to work with paper prints, you need an inclined drawing table with enough space to lay the prints out flat. The table should have a lip on the bottom to keep the prints from sliding off. It should be able to be used from the desk chair without being raised or lowered.

Notes

Plan Racks. Plan racks are used to store drawings and help keep the work area organized. You can make drawing racks yourself that can hold both the drawings and appropriate specifications together.

Printer. A printer that prints double-sided can save a lot of paper when downloading quotes and specifications. In today's construction industry project drawings and specifications are often being distributed electronically and you will have the task of downloading and printing them. There are services available that will download and ship them to you, or you can obtain the equipment to do it yourself. However, the equipment is expensive and time consuming to use.

Scale Ruler. Make sure you have an architectural scale ruler that is based on inches. While not essential, an engineering ruler will make measurements from civil or site drawings easier and more precise.

Software. Good estimating software will take some time to become comfortable with and to master. The amount of time it takes to become adept at using a particular program depends on its complexity and how much time you spend actually using it. The estimated cost for this type of software is $2,000 to $6,000. See Chapter 8 on how to select estimating software.

Telephone and Fax Capabilities. The phone line should be a discreet number for use only by the estimating department. The same holds true for fax capabilities.

Wall Space. A large clear wall in front of your drafting table is convenient for posting important information about the project, but keep this to a minimum or you will end up with clutter.

Whiteboard. A whiteboard can be used for many functions such as scheduling, keeping track of jobs, and so forth. Even if you have a paperless office, such a board is helpful for discussions, temporary notes, and other transient communication activities.

2.4 Types of Bids

There are several types of bid requirements you might experience, and it is imperative that the estimator has a complete grasp of each.

Competitive Bid—Lowest Price

In competitive bidding, the lowest price is sought for a project in a bidding process.

Notes

Design/Build Bid

Design/build bids require the electrical contractor to design and construct the electrical wiring according to written specifications. To be successful with design/build bids, the electrical contractor must know the customer's needs and the *National Electrical Code.*

Negotiated Work

Negotiated work is an agreement reached between the electrical contractor and the customer on the scope of the job and how much it will cost.

Time and Material (Cost Plus)

Time and material pricing is often used when job conditions make it impossible to provide a fixed dollar bid. In its simplest form, price is based on a given rate per labor hour with the material billed at an agreed markup amount (such as 20 percent above cost). This type of work carries a lower risk with a low profit margin; and sometimes it has a "not to exceed" price clause that increases the risk to the contractor, typically with a larger profit margin. This type of work is often used for change orders, especially when a job is over budget.

While some contractors consider this type of work as their "bread and butter," it is more stressful than others because the customer is more likely to question the amount of time for which you bill. It is best to restrict this to customers with whom you have a long term relationship (trust). Also remember that when you do this type of work, it is usually because you are reducing profit in order to reduce risk; adding a "not to exceed" clause adds the risk factor back into the work but the very low profit margin remains, although the risk to accepting such a clause can be reduced when you use unit pricing which we will discuss shortly.

Estimate this type of work as best you can and then stick with the numbers you reached.

Unit Pricing

Some jobs are awarded on the basis of unit pricing (price to install a given electrical component such as a switch, receptacle, or paddle fan) where the unit price includes the cost of labor, material, overhead, and profit. Unit pricing is used for almost all types of construction such as renovations, office build-outs, change orders, and so on. A mistake in a unit price calculation will mean that the mistake in cost will be multiplied by the number of times the unit is used on the project!

Requests for unit pricing are sometimes included in specifications, or in add/deduct options—especially with commercial and residential work. Possible governmental work sometimes consists of an entire (thick) document consisting of nothing but unit pricing items. The low bidder receives a contract for all of the work for a year. Once you receive an order for work to be performed, you can negotiate the price of any additional work/material necessary for "missing" items; such as additional wire for a circuit that must be added because of the number of additional fixtures, receptacles, and/or switches being ordered.

Notes

Author's Comment: In Chapter 7 we will discuss how to determine unit pricing.

2.5 What an Accurate Estimate Must Include

An accurate estimate must include all of the direct costs including; labor (taxes, vacation pay, holiday pay, medical, and retirement), material, sales tax, subcontract and rental expenses, direct job expenses, and overhead.

Author's Comment: Profit is added to the estimate total as the final step before submitting the bid.

2.6 Improper Estimating Methods

Ignoring the Specifications

Plans and specifications work together to communicate the requirements needed to complete the project. The estimator is required to include all of the costs required to comply with them both. Thinking that "you will get away without including a requirement" is not a good strategy if you plan on staying in business.

Ignoring Errors in the Prints and Specifications

With this method, you purposely ignore errors in the prints and specifications, while planning on charging the customer for corrections you knew about ahead of time. This method makes a great way to badger the customer to death for additional money once everyone's committed and the job is under way. A better approach is to compare the specifications to the *National Electrical Code* and other applicable standards and discuss any needed changes with the customer before performing the estimate. This way, you are estimating the actual job instead of the one that will not be done.

Notes

Meeting the Lowest Bid

"Hey, if they can do it for that price, so can I!" Again, not a good business plan.

The "Shot-in-the-Dark" Method

"Let's see, this project has five electrical drawing pages so it should go for about $10,000, yea that's the ticket, $2k per page . . ." With this method, the price can be way out of line, either very high or very low, and you'd better hope you do not get the low-price jobs.

The Square Foot Method

Estimating a job by cost per square foot should actually be considered a "Shot-in-the-Dark" method, although tracking these costs can be a way to help check your estimate.

2.7 The Detailed Estimating Method

The correct method of estimating the cost of a job is the "Detailed Method" and generally includes the following steps:

Step 1: Understanding the Scope of the Bid

The estimator must understand the work to be completed according to the drawings and specifications. Read all of the specifications and make notes of the items that affect the cost. Complete a checklist so you will know when the estimate is done. No guesses here!

Step 2: The Take-Off

A "take-off" is the process of counting and measuring to determine the material needed for the project. When you perform a take-off, you are mentally visualizing the installation of the proposed electrical system and you are counting and measuring the symbols on the drawings. Using a systematic, repetitive system for this step will help keep errors to a minimum. For the person who has the specific electrical experience related to the job, performing the take-off is an easy step and actually very enjoyable, if estimating can be enjoyable.

Step 3: Determining the Bill-of-Material

Information gathered from the take-off is used to create the bill-of-material required for the project. This step is very labor-intensive and lends itself to likely errors. Using a systematic, repetitive system for this step will help keep errors to a minimum.

Author's Comment: If you are using estimating software, most of this will be completed automatically.

Step 4: Pricing and Laboring

Once you have the required bill-of-material list (Step 3), you will need to send it to your supplier(s) for pricing. The labor units for each item must also be looked up in a catalog. This step is fairly easy for experienced electricians because they are familiar with the material; however, most persons can be taught how to perform this process. This is a very labor-intensive step and lends itself to likely errors if done by hand.

Author's Comment: Estimating software will do most of this automatically although labor units for specialty items will still need to be looked up or you will need to request a quotation from suppliers.

Step 5: Extending and Totaling

Once you have the price and labor unit for each item (Step 4), it is time to determine the total material cost and labor. Extending means that the price and labor unit of an item is multiplied by the number of those items taken off. Extending and totaling can be performed by anyone who has reasonable math skills and a calculator. This step is very labor-intensive and lends itself to likely errors if done by hand.

Author's Comment: If you are using estimating software, this will be done automatically.

Step 6: Estimate Summary

Once you have determined the total cost for material and the total labor hours needed, you need to make the necessary adjustment(s) to reflect the job conditions, plus the cost of miscellaneous material and small tools (such as drill bits, screwdrivers, and extension cords), as well as the application of sales tax, subcontractor expenses, direct job costs, and so forth.

Notes

Notes

Step 7: Overhead and Profit

This is where we separate the true estimators from the amateurs. Most electrical contractors can do the take-off and determine the cost of material and labor (if they use labor units), but applying the correct values for overhead, profit, and other final costs is where many contractors fail.

Step 8: Bid Analysis

When the bid is complete, you must verify that you did not make any common estimating errors so you ensure your price is valid and accurate.

Step 9: Proposal

When you have completed the bid, a written proposal must be submitted so there will not be any misunderstandings between you and your customer. The proposal must clearly state what your bid price includes and what it does not include.

2.8 How Accurate Can an Estimate Be?

There is no way to determine with 100 percent accuracy what a job is going to cost, no matter how great you are at estimating. As an estimator, you cannot control variables such as productivity, cost of material, or the activities of other trades; yet, all of these (and more) affect the bottom line. However, you can attempt to predict the cost of these variables with a reasonable level of certainty and accuracy.

So what we must do is anticipate as much as we possibly can so a "projected cost" for the job can be determined. If we estimate correctly and if everything we anticipate happens, we should complete the job reasonably close to our estimated cost.

Not all expenses can be anticipated, but experienced estimators accept a satisfactory margin of error in the accuracy of a bid. As with anything in life, the more experience you have, the more accurate and confident you will become in your bids. With increased experience and practice, you will also increase your speed in completing each estimate.

If you break the job down into its smallest possible parts, then the magnitude of any mistakes will be reduced and they will hopefully cancel each other out (the law of compensating errors). This also helps to keep the guess work to a minimum.

Accuracy of Estimating Material

Notes

Material can be the most predictable part of the estimate, assuming that prices for copper and steel do not skyrocket, and the pricing you used for the estimate was accurate in the first place. Obviously, these prices are effective only during a certain time period and may be subject to change as material costs such as steel and copper fluctuate. During volatile pricing markets, it is very important that the bid includes a time window to address such cost variations. If you are estimating manually, errors in determining the bill-of-material, pricing, extending, and totaling can be significant.

A material budget must be given to the job supervisor to ensure the job is completed as estimated. In addition, we cannot overlook the impact of qualified project management to ensure the job is run according to the estimate.

Author's Comment: The estimator cannot anticipate changes in the wiring by the electrician or unusual waste by the workmen in the field, which can quickly increase the actual cost of the job.

Accuracy of Estimating Labor

Labor is more difficult to predict than material, but with job experience, labor can be calculated to within 10 percent for new work, and 20 percent for remodeling jobs. Keeping a file of completed jobs that are similar can assist in determining the labor adjustments needed in order to be competitive.

A labor budget must be given to the job supervisor to ensure the job is completed as estimated. You cannot overlook the need for qualified project managers to ensure the job is run according to the estimate. In addition, you may need to make adjustments to the estimate based on the expertise or track record of the project manager who will be handling that project so the labor estimate reflects the realities of the job.

Author's Comment: As with material, unusual nonproductive time by the workmen in the field can quickly increase the actual cost of the job.

2.9 Manual Estimate, Estimating Software, or an Estimating Service?

There are three primary methods for effectively estimating a job correctly, with each having its own set of advantages and disadvantages.

Notes

Manual Estimates

Even though manual estimates are good for very small projects, especially if you use unit pricing, and have been sufficient for electrical contractors for over a hundred years, this method is not efficient for the electrical contractor who is regularly bidding jobs. Because it takes so much time to estimate a job manually, you have only enough time to get the bottom line price and not much more. Manual estimating requires so much time that estimates often become backlogged and project management suffers. Additional disadvantages include:

Overhead. No matter how we look at it, estimating a job takes time and costs money. Let's assume we are a small contractor and we win one job out of every four bids we submit. If we successfully win 1 job out of every 4 bids we submit (25%) and we spend an average of 4 hours to estimate each job at $30 per hour (including benefits), it will cost us $480 for every job that we win [4 hrs x 4 jobs = 16 hrs x $30]. If we are able to reduce the amount of time spent on each bid, then the overhead cost per bid will also decrease and that is where computer estimating software shines.

Bid Accuracy. The pressure of completing the estimate quickly so you can move on to the next estimate can result in increased errors as you work with the many calculations involved, especially when there are last minute changes on the bid.

Bill-of-Material. It will not be easy to develop the bill-of-material that you will need to send to your suppliers for pricing and to the job foreman for project management.

Project Management. Because of the time it takes to manually extract project management information without the use of estimating software, most electrical contractors just do not do it. The result is that the job cannot be tracked to ensure it is properly managed.

Response to Changes. It will be very difficult to cope with last minute changes to the drawings or specifications. Sometimes the change is so great that you do not have enough time to redo the bid in a timely manner. This can result in an attempt to make an educated guess, or you may just give up and not submit a bid at all. Either way, this is not a good business practice.

Time. Today, more than any other time in history, we operate in an age of instant information and expected response. Because of cell phones, e-mail, the Internet, and fax machines, customers demand and expect to receive information almost instantaneously. In today's fast-paced world, few customers are willing to give you the time you need to prepare an accurate manual bid.

Estimating Software

The computer-assisted method of estimating is actually the same as estimating manually, except that a computer performs the mathematical calculations. While considerable effort and progress is being made to produce an estimating system that can produce a reliable bill-of-material from a set of drawings, that has yet to be accomplished. However, there are systems now that provide for on-screen take-offs. It must be understood that computer-assisted estimating is only as good as the person's experience in using the system. The many advantages of using estimating software include:

Notes

Overhead. The cost of producing an estimate is an overhead cost. No matter how we look at it, estimating a job takes time and costs money. Let's assume we are a small contractor and we win one job out of every two bids (50%) we submit. We spend an average of 4 hours estimating each job, and the labor rate for the estimator is $30 per hour (including benefits). Based on this information, it will cost us $240 for every job that we win [4 hrs x 2 = 8 hrs x $30].

Bid Accuracy. With estimating software, errors with pricing material and the application of labor units will be significantly reduced, as compared to the manual method. There are no transpositions of numbers, no mistakes on the totals, and no errors when transferring numbers to the estimate summary. Your bids will be clearer, more legible, and more professional in appearance. Estimates will not become backlogged and you will not feel the pressure to rush the estimate, especially with last minute fixture quotes, switchgear quotes, or changes.

Bill-of-Material. Estimating software automatically provides a list of material needed for supplies and project management.

Project Management. Estimating software produces reports with information that can be used for job management, job tracking, and bid analysis. This lends itself to fewer errors before the bid is submitted and allows closer monitoring of field costs as compared to estimated costs as the job progresses.

Response to Changes. It will be easier to accommodate last minute changes to the drawings or specifications.

Time. Estimating software permits you to produce up to four times as many estimates in the same amount of time required to produce one manually. What takes 8 hours manually can take less than 2 hours with a computer and the odds of winning the job are increased.

Estimating Service

An estimating service is a temporary agency that you use and pay for only when you need it. When an estimating service produces an estimate, you have the opportunity to review the information to ensure that the estimate is accurate and complete.

Notes

You might use an estimating service to double-check an estimate you have completed, or when you do not have the time to do it yourself. An estimating service is an excellent tool to help you gain estimating experience at a reduced risk.

Estimating services offer:

Low Up-Front Cost. You can enjoy the benefits of computer-assisted estimates without investing in your own computer estimating system.

Knowing Your Estimate Cost. With an estimating service, you will know in advance what it costs to estimate a job. Their fees are generally based on the total electrical bid dollar amount.

Summary

CHAPTER 2

Notes

2.1 Qualities of a Good Estimator

The following is a list of qualities that identify a good estimator:

- A positive mental attitude
- Computer literacy
- A willingness to learn from one's mistakes
- Familiarity with new products and installation methods
- An understanding of construction and the ability to visualize the electrical requirements
- An orderly mind with a tendency to be careful, accurate, and neat
- Decisiveness and the ability to make decisions without being intimidated by details
- Fairness, honesty, and integrity
- Knowledge of the *National Electrical Code* and local electrical codes
- Patience to finish the estimate without frustration
- Organization
- A willingness to put in whatever time is necessary to meet the bid date and time deadlines

2.2 Duties and Responsibilities of the Estimator

To prepare an estimate properly, you must have the ability to mentally visualize the material items required and how they are installed to complete the job. Because electrical work is complex, the estimator needs to have electrical construction experience (preferably as an electrician).

He or she must be able to envision the need for use of special equipment and/or services that will be required such as scaffolding, man lifts, cranes, trenching, rigging services, and so forth, and include them in the estimate.

Not only do you need to know what is required to complete the job, you must be comfortable with numbers and math as they pertain to *NEC* electrical construction and design calculations. Besides determining the cost of the job, the electrical estimator is often responsible for material purchases and project management information and tracking.

Notes

2.3 The Estimating Workspace and Tools

The Workspace. You need to have the proper workspace and tools with appropriate lighting. The workspace must be laid out efficiently and be located where the estimator will not be disturbed. It needs to be of adequate size, not just a closet with a desk. The workspace should be designed so that everything is within reach from the sitting position.

Estimating Tools. We all know that performing a job without the proper tools often gives poor results, causes frustration, and takes longer than necessary. Proper estimating tools reduce human errors, increase efficiency, and quickly pay for themselves.

2.4 Types of Bids

There are several types of bid requirements you might experience, and it is imperative that the estimator has a complete grasp of each. Types of bids include:

- Competitive Bid—Lowest Price
- Design/Build Bid
- Negotiated Work
- Time and Material (Cost Plus)
- Unit Pricing

2.5 What an Accurate Estimate Must Include

An accurate estimate must include all of the direct costs including; labor (taxes, vacation pay, holiday pay, medical, and retirement), material, sales tax, subcontract and rental expenses, direct job expenses, and overhead.

2.6 Improper Estimating Methods

Improper estimating methods include:

- Ignoring the specifications
- Ignoring errors in the prints and specifications
- Meeting the lowest bid
- The "Shot-in-the-Dark" method
- The Square-Foot method

2.7 The Detailed Estimating Method

Notes

The correct method of estimating the cost of a job is the "Detailed Method" and generally includes the following steps:

- Step 1: Understanding the Scope of the Bid
- Step 2: The Take-Off
- Step 3: Determining the Bill-of-Material
- Step 4: Pricing and Laboring
- Step 5: Extending and Totaling
- Step 6: Estimate Summary
- Step 7: Overhead and Profit
- Step 8: Bid Analysis
- Step 9: Proposal

2.8 How Accurate Can an Estimate Be?

There is no way to determine with 100 percent accuracy what a job is going to cost, no matter how great you are at estimating. As an estimator, you cannot control variables such as productivity, cost of material, or the activities of other trades; yet, all of these (and more) affect the bottom line.

If you break the job down into its smallest possible parts, then the magnitude of any mistakes will be reduced and they will hopefully cancel each other out (the law of compensating errors). This also helps to keep the guess work to a minimum.

Accuracy of Estimating Material. Material can be the most predictable part of the estimate, assuming that prices for copper and steel do not skyrocket, and the pricing you used for the estimate was accurate in the first place.

Accuracy of Estimating Labor. Labor is more difficult to predict than material, but with experience, labor can be calculated to within 10 percent for new work, and 20 percent for remodeling jobs.

2.9 Manual Estimate, Estimating Software, or an Estimating Service?

There are three primary methods for effectively estimating a job:

- Manual Estimates
- Estimating Software
- Estimating Service

CHAPTER 2

Conclusion

Notes

You began this chapter with an understanding of why estimating is important. You have completed it with an understanding of several of the key concepts of estimating. You know what is required of you to be a good estimator and what resources you need to complete good estimates.

Sometimes, you will have to dig for information because you must nail down at the outset what the job actually entails. Armed with that information, there is no reason for you to engage in bad practices, such as meeting the lowest bid. Earlier, we said that estimating does not mean guessing. Begin with the job specifications and use any additional resources necessary to determine what is required to complete that job.

Now that you know the major steps in the estimating process, you are ready to look more closely at how to complete those steps. One of the major components of any electrical job is labor. So we will look at labor units next.

Essay Questions

CHAPTER 2

Notes

1. What are the qualities of a good estimator?

2. What are the general responsibilities of the electrical estimator?

3. Why is it important to have proper workspace and the proper estimating tools?

4. It is imperative that the estimator have a complete grasp on which types of bids?

5. What must an accurate estimate include?

6. What are five improper estimating methods?

Notes

7. What is the proper method of estimating?

8. When estimating a job, what is the best way to reduce the magnitude of any mistakes and keep guess work to a minimum?

9. What are the three primary methods for estimating a job?

Multiple-Choice Questions

CHAPTER 2

Notes

2.1 Qualities of a Good Estimator

1. A good estimator only needs knowledge of the *National Electrical Code*.

   (a) True
   (b) False

2.2 Duties and Responsibilities of the Estimator

2. Because electrical work is complex, the estimator needs to have electrical construction experience (preferably as a(n) ______).

   (a) electrician
   (b) apprentice electrician
   (c) journeyman electrician
   (d) master electrician

3. Besides determining the cost of the job, the electrical estimator is often responsible for ______.

   (a) material purchases
   (b) project management information and tracking
   (c) a and b
   (d) none of these

2.3 The Estimating Workspace and Tools

4. Before you even think of estimating a job, you need to have ______.

   (a) the proper workspace
   (b) the proper tools
   (c) appropriate lighting
   (d) all of these

Notes

5. Proper estimating tools ______.

(a) reduce human errors
(b) increase efficiency
(c) quickly pay for themselves
(d) all of these

2.4 Types of Bids

6. In ______ bidding, the lowest price is sought for a project in a bidding process.

(a) negotiated
(b) design/build
(c) competitive
(d) time and material

7. ______ bids require the electrical contractor to design and construct the electrical wiring according to written specifications.

(a) Negotiated
(b) Design/build
(c) Competitive
(d) Time and material

8. ______ work is an agreement reached between the electrical contractor and the customer on the scope of the job and how much it will cost.

(a) Negotiated
(b) Design/build
(c) Competitive
(d) Time and material

9. ______ pricing is often used when job conditions make it impossible to provide a fixed dollar bid.

(a) Negotiated
(b) Design/build
(c) Competitive
(d) Time and material

Notes

10. Some jobs are awarded on the basis of unit pricing (price to install a given electrical component) where the unit price includes the cost of labor, material, overhead, and profit.

    (a) True
    (b) False

2.5 What an Accurate Estimate Must Include

11. An accurate estimate must include all of the direct costs including; labor (taxes, vacation pay, holiday pay, medical, and retirement), material, sales tax, subcontract and rental expenses, direct job expenses, and ______.

    (a) overhead
    (b) profit
    (c) a and b
    (d) a or b

2.6 Improper Estimating Methods

12. Thinking that "you will get away without including a requirement" from the ______ is not a good strategy if you plan on staying in business.

    (a) plans
    (b) specifications
    (c) a and b
    (d) a or b

13. The estimating method that makes a great way to badger the customer to death for additional money once everyone's committed and the job is under way is called "______."

    (a) ignoring errors in the prints and specifications
    (b) meeting the lowest bid
    (c) the "Shot-in-the-Dark" method
    (d) all of these

Notes

2.7 The Detailed Estimating Method

14. Read all of the specifications and make notes of the items that affect the cost. Complete a ______ so you will know when the estimate is done.

    (a) job folder
    (b) checklist
    (c) worksheet
    (d) none of these

15. A(n) "______" is the process of counting and measuring to determine the material needed for the project.

    (a) estimate
    (b) bid
    (c) take-off
    (d) bill-of-material

16. Information gathered from the ______ is used to create the ______ required for the project.

    (a) take-off, estimate
    (b) bid, bill-of-material
    (c) bill-of-material, take-off
    (d) take-off, bill-of material

17. Pricing and laboring is fairly easy for experienced electricians because they are familiar with the material.

    (a) True
    (b) False

18. Extending and totaling is very labor-intensive and lends itself to likely errors if done by hand.

    (a) True
    (b) False

Notes

19. Once you have determined the total cost for material and the total labor hours needed, you must apply labor burden.

(a) True
(b) False

20. Applying the correct values for ______ is where many contractors fail.

(a) overhead
(b) profit
(c) other final costs
(d) all of these

2.8 How Accurate Can an Estimate Be?

21. As an estimator, you cannot control variables such as ______.

(a) productivity
(b) cost of material
(c) the activities of other trades
(d) all of these

22. A material budget must be given to the ______ to ensure the job is completed as estimated.

(a) general contractor
(b) inspector
(c) job supervisor
(d) customer

23. Labor is more difficult to predict than material, but with experience, labor can be calculated to within ______ percent for new work, and ______ percent for remodeling jobs.

(a) 5, 15
(b) 10, 20
(c) 15, 25
(d) 20, 30

Notes

2.9 Manual Estimate, Estimating Software, or an Estimating Service?

24. Manual estimating requires so much ______ that estimates often become backlogged and project management suffers.

    (a) paperwork
    (b) time
    (c) a and b
    (d) none of these

25. ______ is only as good as the person's experience in using the system.

    (a) Manual estimating
    (b) An estimating service
    (c) Computer-assisted estimating
    (d) none of these

26. ______ is a temporary agency that you use and pay for only when you need it.

    (a) Manual estimating
    (b) An estimating service
    (c) Computer-assisted estimating
    (d) none of these

CHAPTER

3 UNDERSTANDING LABOR UNITS

INTRODUCTION

When you do an electrical estimate, two of the major cost components of the job you will need to determine include material/equipment and labor. The labor component is where the estimate is most likely to go wrong, and where errors can do the greatest damage to the project.

To estimate labor requirements, you start with standard labor-unit guides that tell you how many labor hours it should take to do a certain task under "typical" job conditions (for example, run 100 ft of trade size 1 EMT). Many factors can increase job difficulty, so you must examine the actual conditions of the job you are estimating and adjust the labor hours accordingly. Some labor variables are specific to the site (location, security access, customer procedures, and so forth), whereas some are specific to the crew selection (Harry works at a faster pace than average, Tim works at a slower pace than average).

Experience can help you adjust labor units more accurately, but do not let experience give you a false sense of confidence; do not use it "instead of" the labor-units method.

To drive home that point, consider the following labor variables: working height, the location of stairs, the distance from the parking area, temperature considerations (extreme heat or cold), crowding factors (how many other trades there are), shift work, repetitive task issues, the extent of ladder and scaffold use, the distance from your home base, the availability of adequate labor and material, as well as electric power.

Experience can be personal (belonging to you or people you know) or organizational (belonging to the company). Both can help, but only if you do not rely too heavily on them. Let's look briefly at each one:

Personal experience provides a "feel" for what it takes to do a job. Keep in mind that one's memory has a way of changing "the facts" over time. It follows from this that you should use personal experience as a way to check your estimated labor requirements, not as a way to determine them.

Organizational experience, for a contracting company, exists in the records of past jobs. If they are similar to the one you are estimating, you can carry over much of the information to the new job.

The approach of using labor units takes more time than trying to guess how long it will take to do the job, but doing so reduces the likelihood of errors and oversights. Just one error can turn a profit-promising job into a money-losing job.

Notes

3.1 What Is a Labor Unit?

A labor unit represents the approximate amount of time required to install an electrical product, component, or piece of equipment. Labor units are based on the assumption that a highly trained, skilled, and motivated electrician is completing the task under a "specific" set of installation conditions, and using the proper tools and supervision.

Typical Project

The following general description defines a typical project for the purposes of estimating using labor units:

- **Building Size and Shape.** Up to three floors above street level, 20,000 to 100,000 square feet per floor, with a rectangular or square floor plan.
- **Construction and Work Schedule.** Standard workday, 40 hours per workweek, daylight shift, time to eliminate scheduled overtime, and with no more than 100 qualified electricians on the job.
- **Location.** In or near a metropolitan area, outside of a controlled access area, and a single building, facility, or activity.
- **Systems.** Electrical service by the utility, new listed material, and not more than 20 feet above a solid floor.

Typical Site Conditions

Typical site conditions for the purposes of estimating using labor units are generally described as follows:

- Adequate security for material and tool storage
- All electrical material furnished by the electrical contractor
- All new material and new construction
- Complete engineering, with well-coordinated design, drawings, and specifications
- Crane furnished by others
- Familiar type of building design and standard material
- Few interruptions or delays
- Minimum quantity and magnitude of change orders
- Minimum temperature of 35°F, maximum temperature of 88°F, and 50 percent relative humidity

- Optimum job coordination of all trades
- Overall job progress based on a realistic project schedule
- Sufficient supply of qualified journeymen electricians

Notes

Labor units must be adjusted for management skill and for any variable conditions on the jobsite. The methods of adjusting labor units are discussed later in this chapter.

3.2 How Labor Units Are Expressed

Labor units are expressed in units of decimal hours with the following letter codes: "E"—each, "C"—hundreds, or "M"—thousands. The reason labor hours are expressed in decimal form is that the hours can be added in a manner similar to dollars and cents, rather than having to add hours and minutes individually.

For example, the labor to install a receptacle is listed as 18/C, which means that 100 receptacles are expected to be installed in 18 hours or 0.18 hours per receptacle (18 hours/100). We can convert 0.18 hours per receptacle into minutes as follows; 60 minutes x 0.18 hours each = 11 minutes.

> **Author's Comment:** It might appear that 11 minutes to install a duplex receptacle is way too much time, and you will never win a job if you use labor units, but that is really not the case.

3.3 Using Work Experience

Electrical work experience is important when you estimate electrical wiring, but you must know when and how to use that experience. Many electrical contractors estimate a job based on how long they think it will take them to do it. There are other factors that should also be taken into consideration, such as supervision, job layout, the handling of tools and material, nonproductive time, and variable job conditions.

Work experience is important, as a matter of fact it is critical, but it should not be the basis you use to estimate a job. If you could simply estimate the labor of a job with your experience, you probably would not be reading this book.

Meeting Room Labor Hours

How many labor hours do you think it will take to complete the wiring for the Meeting Room Drawing M–1? Figure 3–1

Notes

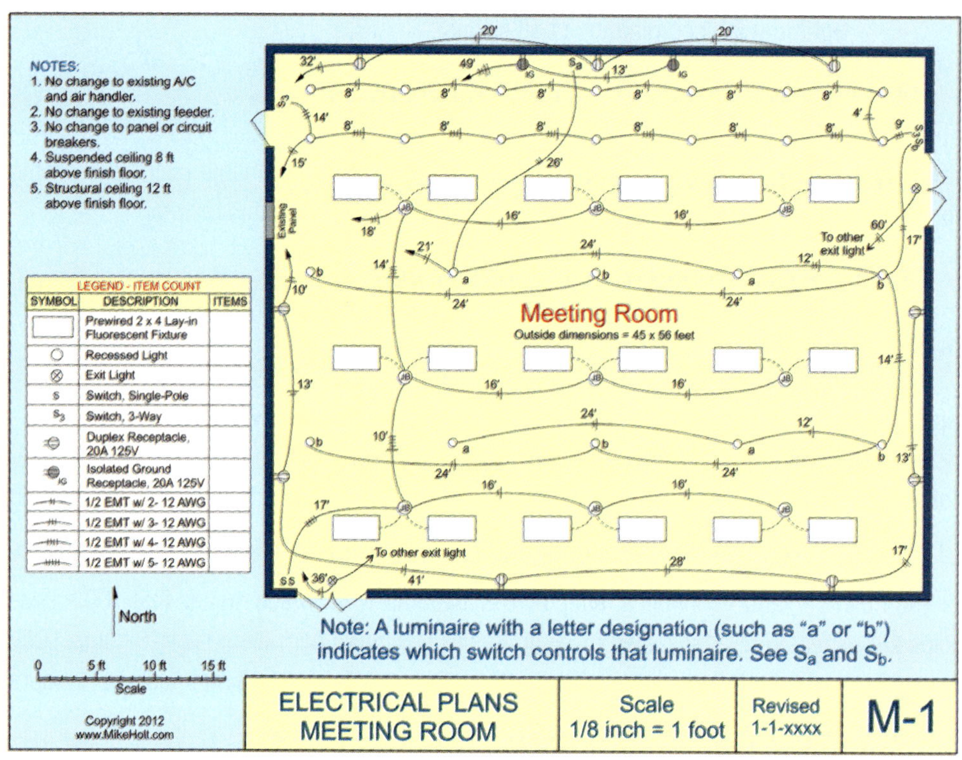

Figure 3–1

I have asked over 1,000 master electricians in my classes to estimate the labor hours required to rough in and trim the meeting room. The answers range from a low of 40 hours to over 200 hours. If you like, show the plan to five electricians and ask them what they think and you will see what I mean.

> **Author's Comment:** Differences in estimated labor hours is one of the reasons there is such a vast variation in pricing between electrical contractors.

Based on NECA labor units, the estimated labor hours for the Meeting Room will be 82.84 hours (see the following table). Some electrical contractors will be more efficient and organized and complete the project in less time, whereas other electrical contractors are so disorganized that they will be lucky to finish it in less than 125 hours.

Meeting Room Labor Unit					
Description	Qty	Hours	Unit	Ext Hrs	Calculation
Boxes					
Metal Boxes 4 x 4" Regular	30	18.00	C/100	5.40	18 hr/100 x 30
Rings					
Rings, Square Round	6	4.50	C/100	0.27	4.50 hr/100 x 6
Rings, 1-Gang	13	4.50	C/100	0.59	4.50 hr/100 x 13
Rings, 2-Gang	2	5.00	C/100	0.10	5 hr/100 x 2
Switches					
Switch - 20A, 125/277V, 1-Pole	4	20.00	C/100	0.80	20 hr/100 x 4
Switch - 20A, 125/277V, 3-Way	2	25.00	C/100	0.50	25 hr/100 x 2
Receptacles					
Duplex Receptacle 20A, 125V	9	19.00	C/100	1.71	19 hr/100 x 9
Isolated Ground Receptacle 20A, 120V	2	0.25	E/Each	0.50	0.25 hr x 2
Plates					
Plates, Plastic 1-Gang Switch	2	2.50	C/100	0.05	2.50 hr/100 x 2
Plates, Plastic 2-Gang Switch	2	4.00	C/100	0.08	4 hr/100 x 2
Plates, Plastic 1-Gang Duplex Receptacle	11	2.50	C/100	0.28	2.50 hr/100 x 11
Plates, Raised 4 x 4" Blank	9	6.00	C/100	0.54	6 hr/100 x 9
Raceway					
EMT ½"	891	2.25	C/100	20.05	2.25 hr/100 x 891
EMT Set Screw Connectors ½"	100	2.00	C/100	2.00	2 hr/100 x 100
EMT Set Screw Couplings ½"	90	2.00	C/100	1.80	2 hr/100 x 90
Wire					
Wire - 12 THHN, Copper, 600V	2,393	4.25	M/1,000	10.17	4.25 hr/1000 x 2,393
Fixtures					
4' Fluorescent Lay-In, 2 Lamps, 120V	18	0.75	E/Each	13.50	0.75 hr x 18
Recessed Fixture	24	1.00	E/Each	24.00	1 hr x 24
Exit Fixture	2	0.25	E/Each	0.50	0.25 hr x 2
Total Labor-Unit Hours				**82.84**	

Notes

Notes

3.4 What Is Included in the Labor Unit?

A labor unit has six major components: job installation, job layout, material handling and cleanup, nonproductive labor, supervision, and tool handling and safety. Figure 3–2

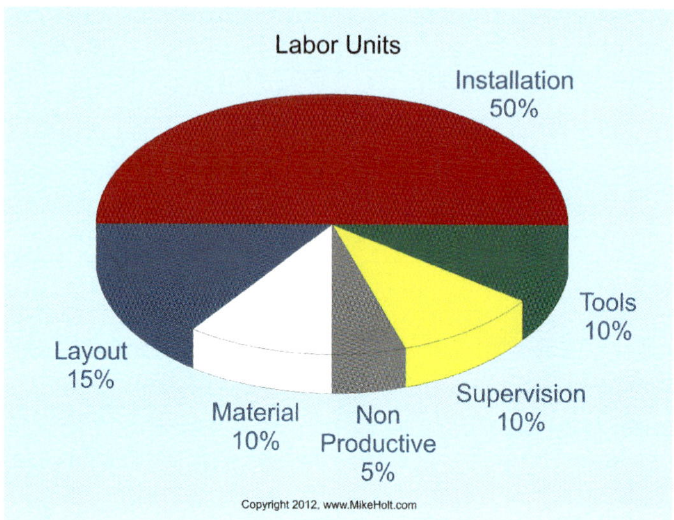

Figure 3–2

1. Installation (50 Percent)

The actual installation time only represents about 50 percent of the labor unit. This includes the physical time it should take to install boxes, conduit, fittings, wiring devices, fixtures, switchgear, disconnects, panels, breakers, and so forth. Be sure you always provide the proper tools so the installation can be completed in the most efficient manner.

2. Job Layout (15 Percent)

The layout of the work represents 15 percent of the labor unit. This includes measuring and determining the type, size, and location of the raceways, wire, cables, boxes, circuits, fixtures, and so on.

3. Material Handling and Cleanup (10 Percent)

Material handling and cleanup represents 10 percent of the labor unit. Do not forget you must unpack, receive, count, unload, store material, and dispose of the packing containers in which the items were shipped.

Notes

4. Nonproductive Labor (5 Percent)

All jobs include nonproductive labor, which should be managed so as not to exceed 5 percent of the labor unit.

Author's Comment: Be careful of long breaks and early quitting time—which are often linked with late starting time. You know how it goes; two guys look at their watches, one watch indicates 8:00 a.m., and the other shows 7:55 a.m. Of course they wait 5 minutes to start the job. The opposite is true at the end of the day. This game results in a loss of 10 minutes a day per electrician.

5. Supervision (10 Percent)

Supervision represents 10 percent of the labor unit. It includes reviewing the drawings and specifications, ordering material, working out installation problems, coordinating with other trades and subcontractors, inspection tours, record keeping for material, job progress reports, time cards, and a ton of other things.

6. Tool Handling (10 Percent)

The management, handling, and layout of tools represent 10 percent of the labor unit. Somebody must receive, store, move, set up, remove, and clean the tools!

3.5 Labor Units Do Not Include

Labor units do not include the assembly of fixtures or equipment supplied by others. Be careful when the owner supplies the fixtures, or when you receive very low prices from your supplier for fixtures or gear. The equipment might come in a bag with assembly instructions. Other factors that are not included in a labor unit are:

- Cutting holes or openings
- Excavation, drilling, or blasting
- Heavy equipment operators' time
- Hoisting material and equipment above three floors
- Maintenance of temporary equipment
- Painting of conduits
- Patching or painting
- Testing or welding
- Sealing fire-rated penetrations

Notes

Preassembled Equipment

Whenever possible, purchase preassembled equipment or equipment that is installer-friendly. Equipment that is not preassembled will cost you more by the time you put it together.

For example, order lay-in fixtures that are pre-lamped and pre-whipped. For larger installations, order feeder conductors for long pulls in triplex or quadplex on a single reel. This is a real time saver because the wire is already together and you are only pulling from one reel. The cost of triplex or quadplex might be slightly greater, but the labor savings will exceed the increased material cost.

Unusual Tasks

There will be times when you must determine the amount of labor needed for a task that you have absolutely no idea of how to approach. What you need to do is break the task down into as many small individual labor segments as possible. Try to establish a labor unit for each segment by comparing the individual segments to a similar task that you do have a labor unit for. If all else fails, make an educated guess based on experience and prior knowledge.

Author's Comment: If your employees are not familiar with a particular type of wiring, the labor required to manage, install, and troubleshoot that system will be significantly increased.

3.6 Labor-Unit Manuals

You must purchase a comprehensive labor-unit manual that contains at least 10,000 labor units. Excellent labor-unit manuals are available in both book form and electronically from NECA and www.MikeHolt.com. Also, be sure to stick to labor units shown in a single manual for the entire job because they are developed in a coordinated manner.

There is no perfect set of labor units that can be applied to all jobs by all electrical contractors. With experience and historical data, you will develop techniques to help you adjust the labor units so they represent your productivity under specific job conditions.

3.7 How to Develop Your Own Labor Units

You will really not develop your own labor units, what you will develop is the "labor-unit adjustment" you will apply to adjust the labor units you are using. To determine your "labor-unit adjustments," compare the estimated hours of a job against the actual number of hours it took. After tracking a few jobs, you will learn what your "adjustment" is for the next job, based on the labor units that you are using.

Notes

Author's Comment: If you do not manage your job properly, your actual labor hours will likely exceed the estimate. If your labor-unit adjustment reflects your inefficiency, your bids will not be as competitive as they can be.

3.8 Your Labor Units as Compared to Your Competitors

Productivity in the installation of electrical equipment is affected by many factors, and the most significant is project management. If the actual labor exceeds the estimate, the primary cause is usually a deficiency in project management. This is because management determines the labor budget, the level of supervision, and whether the labor force is skilled and motivated enough to be sufficiently productive. Management is also responsible for having the proper tools and material on the job at the right time.

1. Project Management Information

The estimate must provide the estimated labor hour/cost budget for each phase of the job (slab, rough in, trim). With this information, the electricians in the field have a basis to know how many hours it should take to complete a given portion of the project. If you and the field workers do not know how long it should take to complete a project, you will never know if your labor is productive, and you will not be able to move the project to completion in a profitable manner. It is also a good idea to assign tasks to your workers that they like to do and at which they excel. They will be happier and more productive.

2. Labor Skill Level

Labor units are based on the assumption that highly trained, skilled, and motivated electricians are completing the task. Some electrical contractors "save money" by using an unskilled and unmotivated labor force (which is less productive and more prone to costly errors), while other electrical contractors cultivate a highly skilled and motivated team that will get the job done. The skill and motivation of your labor force will affect your labor productivity. You know the saying, "You get what you pay for."

Training. Do you have an ongoing training program? Do you send your employees to school to learn about changes to the *National Electrical Code*? Are your field and office staff taught and shown ways to become more productive and customer responsive? If you fail an inspection, do you review the *Code* violations with the electricians so they will not make the same mistakes again?

Notes

Be sure your employees are properly trained in advance in all aspects of their job including safety, the proper use of tools, the *NEC*, and efficient work practices. The investment in training is offset by increased labor productivity, reduced down-time due to accidents or injuries, and reduced callbacks or rework.

Experience. With experience, workers can complete a project more quickly. If you estimate jobs with which you have experience, you should have a more competitive labor unit, as opposed to jobs with which you have little or no experience.

> ***Example:*** *In tract housing, experienced electrical contractors can beat the labor units used in this textbook by as much as 40 percent and still make money, whereas a commercial electrical contractor (having never done houses) will be lucky to break even, without any labor-unit adjustment.*

3. Material and Tools

To complete a project efficiently, you must have the material and tools, and all pertinent information, on the job when they are needed. If they are not, then your labor force will be wasting your money trying to find something to do. Whose fault is this? Remember, labor units are based on a skilled electrician utilizing the most current labor-saving tools. If you do not provide proper tools and the training on the safe use of those tools, your labor force will not be as productive.

Author's Comment: Make sure the tools are always properly maintained and are in a safe working condition.

4. Supervision/Project Management

If you want to make money, be sure you use a qualified management team to manage the job according to the estimate.

3.9 Knowing Your Competitors' Labor Units

It does not help you to know the labor units your competitors use because your style of management, your organizational strengths and weaknesses, and the skill of your labor force are all unique to your company. To be competitive, you must continue to strive to improve efficiency and effectiveness as an electrical contractor. Do not worry about your competitors, you have enough problems of your own to work on.

Notes

3.10 Variables That Affect Labor Units

Remember—there is no set of labor units that fits all jobs. Data from a labor-unit manual must be adjusted to fit the job conditions that you are dealing with. Some job variables can be controlled, whereas others must be accepted as a cost of doing business. The adjustment factors that we will be discussing are only a suggested guide. You must keep historical information on past jobs so you can develop your own adjustments. Keep in mind that you will probably only have a few of these variables on any one job.

At some point in your career, you will need to consider some (if not all) of the following factors when adjusting labor units for job conditions.

1. Building Conditions

Identical electrical material used in different types of buildings and projects may require either more or less labor to install than the average labor units. The major reasons include building complexity, floor conditions, hoisting restrictions, and working height.

Complexity. Job complexity can cause confusion and often requires greater supervision, so you need to be alert to this condition. For example, it takes more time to run 100 ft of trade size ¾ EMT in an existing research laboratory than it does to run it down the wall of an unfinished office.

Floor Conditions. If the floor area is covered with sheets of plywood, wood, garbage, or even rain water, you can bet that it is going to take your staff more time to complete the installation. Some general contractors require the subcontractors to clean up after themselves so that the next trade has a clean working area, whereas other general contractors let this issue resolve itself between the subcontractors.

Hoisting Restrictions. In some high-rise buildings, elevators or cranes can only be used to transport construction material during certain hours of the day, so be sure to coordinate the movement of material and tools so that you do not have electricians standing around waiting for them. Some projects will require that material be moved only during off-hours, so the additional costs for premium time need to be included in your bid.

Working Height. Labor units are based on buildings and projects with up to three floors above grade or street level. As the number of floors increase, there is an increase in the number of labor hours needed to move equipment, material, tools, and labor to the work area. In addition, the need to wait for the lifts at the start of the day, end of the day, for breaks, lunch, and so on, increases the number of labor hours that will be required.

Notes

Single-Floor Adjustment. Add 1 percent for the single floor level you are working on. For example, if you are doing a build-out on the ninth floor, increase your total labor by 9 percent.

> **Author's Comment:** NECAnet.org has a research report entitled *The Effect of Multi-Story Buildings on Productivity.*

Entire Building Adjustment. When wiring the entire building, the following adjustment factors apply to the total building labor hours for buildings with repetitive floor drawings.

Wiring the Entire Building Labor Adjustments	
1 to 2 Floors	0%
3 to 6 Floors	1%
7 to 8 Floors	2%
9 to 14 Floors	5%
15 to 19 Floors	7%
20 to 30 Floors	13%

> **Author's Comment:** The reason these percentages appear low is because each floor in the building is similar and you gain labor productivity due to repetition.

2. Change Orders

Jobs are rarely completed as originally planned; revisions to the electrical system are often required to accommodate changes in the building design or to accommodate a change in the owner's needs. Change orders often result in a delay in the job schedule for all trades, which in itself can decrease the labor productivity of your staff. Because change orders often affect the planning or scheduling of work, those in the field sometimes develop a negative work ethic and unfavorable worker attitude toward the project.

Other monetary factors you should consider when dealing with change orders include increased overhead cost, interruption of job flow, the effect on labor of compressing the job schedule, overtime, revisions to as-built drawings, increased project management cost, and possible restocking charges from your suppliers for returned items. If the schedule is delayed there are other unexpected costs, such as increased financing cost, storage cost, supervision cost, and so forth, which must be recovered.

There are no specific labor adjustments you can add to a job for anticipated change orders. The best you can do is be aware of the impact on the estimated job labor. You might need to add additional labor when pricing the change order to compensate for the loss in productivity it causes to the original contract.

Notes

Author's Comment: NECAnet.org has a research report entitled *Impact of Change Orders on Labor Efficiency for Electrical Construction.*

3. Contractor Management Skill

Labor units are based on the effective coordination and management of the project by the contractor or construction manager. If the project is not managed effectively by the contractor, productivity losses will occur. Losses can occur because of:

- An accelerated construction schedule
- Excessive change orders
- Material furnished by the owner
- Overtime to maintain the construction schedule
- Poor coordination of subcontractors
- The redesign of any part of a project after construction has started
- Starting construction without complete or coordinated construction drawings

Be sure you consider the general contractor's management effectiveness, and adjust the labor hours when necessary.

4. Embedded and Exposed Wiring

Embedded Wiring. When installing wiring systems such as boxes and raceway systems in concrete or masonry portions of a building, you need to realize that they often require significantly more labor as compared to installing the same wiring concealed in a drywall partition. Consider applying the following adjustments for concealed wiring:

Embedded Wiring Labor Adjustments	
Boxes/raceways in walls	50%
Boxes/raceways in columns	100%

Notes

Exposed Wiring. Installing exposed wiring methods such as boxes and raceways requires more installation time in order to do nice offsets and ensure that the pipe is installed parallel and level along the building lines. Where multiple raceways are run next to each other, each must be carefully bent so they are run symmetrically. Consider applying the following labor adjustments to that portion of the wiring method that will be exposed:

Exposed Wiring Labor Adjustments	
Boxes	10%
Raceways	20%

5. Job Factors

Labor units are based on typical job locations that do not include any unusual problems. When a project location creates unusual material and tool handling issues, any other type of physical obstructions, or administrative obstructions, productivity losses must be considered. Some of the abnormal conditions that may cause productivity losses include:

- Delivery restrictions
- Dispersed work areas
- Hoisting restrictions
- Lack of space for a job shed
- Parking restrictions and availability
- Security restrictions
- Security problems
- Storage restrictions

Productivity losses due to abnormal job conditions must be determined by judgment, logic, and common sense.

If the job is remote from the office, the challenge for the office to ensure that the job is managed effectively increases. Sometimes a job located in a remote location is forgotten or ignored by the electrical contractor with disastrous results. Be careful when estimating the labor requirements for an "out-of-town job" that requires you to hire local electricians for a temporary period of time. Will the pay scale be higher than it is in your immediate area? How productive or loyal do you think the workers will be?

> **Author's Comment:** Be sure to include travel time to the jobsite in the estimate if required. You may also need to include lodging and other related costs for your staff if the site is far enough away from your home office.

You will need to increase your labor units for small jobs (such as remodel work) because you cannot gain any labor savings due to repetition and economies of scale. How much do you adjust? Since there is no standard adjustment factor for this type of situation, track your actual labor against your estimates for past jobs to see what pattern develops.

Notes

6. Labor Skill

Labor units are based on having an adequate supply of qualified electricians, and not having them results in a loss of productivity that must be taken into consideration during the estimating process. It is impossible to precisely determine that loss, but an attempt must be made based on experience, judgment, and common sense.

Attitude. What is your attitude toward your employees? If you do not treat them with respect, you will have high turnover and low productivity rates. If you treat them well, pay them fairly, give them all of the benefits you can afford, and provide and pay for continuing education, you will have dedicated employees who will do all they can to complete the job in an efficient and effective manner.

Experience and Skill. A well-paid, motivated, qualified, highly trained, and experienced electrician will always be more productive than an employee who feels cheated, does not care about the success of your business, and does not feel like part of the team.

If you do not have motivated, skilled, and experienced electricians, the ones you do have will need extra supervision. Poorly skilled labor results in an increase in costs to correct violations and fix mistakes. Your hiring policy will determine the quality of your employees and their attitude, but how you treat them will determine how long they will stay and how productive they will be.

Training. A continuously trained labor force will always be more efficient and productive than an unskilled force. Your investment in continuing education will result in increased labor productivity. Do you have a training program to teach your employees how to be more productive? What about people skills so they understand how to treat each other, the other trades, and customers? If you fail an inspection, do you have a review process so that all staff members know what was wrong so the same mistake is not repeated? Safety training decreases the likelihood of an accident which drives costs up due to down time and increased insurance costs. It also shows that there is concern for your employees and increases production.

Notes

7. Ladder and Scaffold Work

Ladder. Any portion of a job that requires working on a ladder will result in an increase in labor as compared to a job at grade level. Tools and material must be raised to the working area and lowered back down again (not carried up and down the ladder, which is an unsafe practice). Working is more difficult and tiring on a ladder, and there is an increased risk of injury from falls. The following labor-unit adjustments for ladder work should be considered for any portion of the job that is not at grade level.

Ladder Labor-Unit Adjustments	
12 ft	3%
13 ft	5%
14 ft	8%
15 ft	10%
16 ft	13%
17 ft	16%
18 ft	19%
19 ft	22%
20 ft	25%

Scaffold. If you are performing work from a scaffold, you need to consider the labor required to set up, move, and dismantle it. Do not forget you have to somehow get tools and material up to the working platform, then before the scaffold can be moved, all tools, equipment, and material must be brought back down. If in moving the scaffold you encounter a large obstruction (like a doorway), it might have to be disassembled and reassembled. For safety and efficiency, you will need one electrician at the bottom of the scaffold at all times.

How much do you increase the labor unit for work performed on a scaffold? This is a tough one, but figure at least a 40 to 50 percent increase in labor units, plus the time to wrestle with it (setup time, take-down, and the time needed to return the scaffold). If the work can be performed from motorized platform lifts, this adjustment can be significantly reduced.

8. Management

Proper job management ensures a well-trained and motivated quality workforce that has the material, tools, and information needed to get the job done right the first time with the least amount of effort. If properly trained, equipped, and motivated, your work force will be content and proud to work for your company; and that means they will give their best. If you (the

Notes

manager or owner) are not organized, you can be sure that all of those below you are not organized either and will have difficulty competing in today's market.

The most efficient method of having a productive labor force is for them to be happy. Of course, everybody wants a bigger paycheck but that is not all there is to being happy. What people desire is to feel valued and believe they are part of something special.

Successful contractors hire the right people, pay them fairly, provide them with benefits, give them continuing education, and let them know that they are important—but that is just the beginning. Be sure all of your management staff follows your lead. Do not forget to provide supervisory training for them in all aspects of their responsibility including people skills, job budgeting, project management, and time management.

Make sure that you have a high level of communication from the office to the supervisor about the project at hand and about how the job was estimated. Be sure you have meetings between the office and field personnel to review job progress on a regular basis.

9. Material

Planning your material orders is critical to ensure the electricians are not held up due to material shortages. There are hundreds of minor items that your workers can run out of, and any one of them can stop a job in its tracks and cost you money while someone makes a parts run. Remember that if the material is not delivered to the job on time, you will be losing money you did not need to lose. Running out of material on a job destroys continuity and motivation on the job; not to mention the cost of inefficiency.

10. Overtime

Labor units are based on normal work schedules of 8 daylight hours per day, five days per week, and 40 total hours per week, with a minimum amount of overtime once or twice a month. When overtime is required for any reason, there is a substantial loss of productivity during the overtime hours worked, as well as the normal hours preceding overtime.

As overtime increases in magnitude and duration, productivity losses also increase. Overtime interrupts established life patterns and causes fatigue, reduced motivation, and lower productivity. Workers have a tendency to forget safety procedures, which can result in serious accidents and possible fatalities. Consider the following adjustments:

Notes

Overtime Adjustments	
Six 8-Hour Days	
One Week:	+ 15% for the 6th day
Every Week:	+ 15% all labor for week
Saturdays and Sundays after Five Days	
One Weekend:	+ 30% for weekend hours
Every Weekend:	+ 30% all labor for week
Extended Regular Hours	
Six 10-hour days:	+ 18% all labor
Seven 10-hour days:	+ 30% all labor

Author's Comment: NECAnet.org has a research report entitled *Overtime and Productivity in Electrical Construction.*

11. Remodel (Old Work)

The only way you can know what adjustments to apply for remodel work, with any degree of accuracy, is to track the labor of every remodel job you do and compare the actual hours against the labor unit for future reference. Once you have some experience and job history, you will be better prepared to adjust the labor for future projects. But doubling the labor unit for fishing and cutting in boxes is not a bad place to start.

12. Repetitive Factor

When you perform the same function over and over again, you complete the task a little faster than the previous time which can significantly improve your labor productivity. Consider the following labor adjustments if you have any repetitive work:

Repetitive Labor-Unit Adjustments	
1 to 2 Repeats	0%
3 to 5 Repeats	- 15%
6 to 10 Repeats	- 25%
11 to 15 Repeats	- 35%

Notes

13. Restrictive Working Conditions

Sometimes, due to an accelerated schedule, you will have multiple trades working together in the same room or space (stacking). This forces the trades to work around each other, often resulting in conflict and decreased labor productivity.

Author's Comment: The NECA research report, *Factors Affecting Labor Productivity of Electrical Contractors* has a section about the stacking of trades.

14. Schedule

The construction schedule must be taken into consideration when you prepare the estimate. Labor units in all manuals are based on the fact that the job will be properly staffed with sufficient qualified persons, using proper tools, who are properly supervised on a project of normal duration. In addition, labor units are based on the fact that the job will be run in an efficient manner where the employees work no more than 8 hours per day.

When the project follows an abnormal project progress schedule, abnormal project completion date, or when the project progress schedule is substantially revised, there is a loss of productivity. The magnitude of the productivity loss is related to the circumstances of the particular project involved.

Extended-duration jobs resulting from delays due to factors such as weather or poor job management can cause a reduction in labor productivity and an increase in careless mistakes.

Author's Comment: NECAnet.org has a research report entitled *Normal Project Duration.*

Accelerated. A job that is projected to run on an accelerated schedule requires the electrical contractor to have more manpower on-site than would be typical. This applies not only to the electrical contractor but also to the other trades. This can result in the contractor needing to hire "temporary" staff that might not be as well-trained or motivated to produce as the "permanent" staff.

An accelerated production schedule can cause havoc in scheduling material and tools to be on-site when needed and the impact on labor productivity must be taken into consideration when too many workers are in the same area at the same time. Do not forget to consider the negative effects of increased supervision pressure and the possible poor productivity of temporary staff.

There is no specific labor adjustment factor for an accelerated schedule, but you should consider its effect on your labor productivity.

Notes

Example: *What is the crew size for a six-week project that has estimated labor of 1,200 hours?*

Crew Size = Total Hours/Number of Weeks/40 hours per week
Crew Size = 1,200 hours/six weeks/40 hours
Crew Size = Five electricians.

If you accelerate the schedule to three weeks, you will need twice as many electricians, and your labor productivity will likely decrease resulting in an increase in labor cost for the job. You may also have to include overtime to meet the compressed scheduling.

Author's Comment: NECAnet.org has a research report entitled *Project Peak Workforce Report.*

15. Shift Work

When scheduling shift work, take into consideration the lifestyles of your employees. Generally, single employees without parental responsibility prefer to work the second shift (3 p.m. to 11 p.m.), whereas married employees given the choice between second or third shifts, prefer the third shift (11 p.m. to 7 a.m.). But check with each employee and see what they prefer and, where possible, try to accommodate them.

Shift Work Labor Adjustments			
	Overall	**Single**	**Married**
Second Shift	20 to 25%	15 to 20%	25 to 30%
Third Shift	15 to 20%	20 to 25%	15 to 20%

16. Teamwork

If the general contractor does not coordinate effectively, that deficiency is going to cause everyone problems and probably cost you money. When there is stress between the various trades, you can expect problems and a reduction in labor productivity. When possible, try to stimulate and encourage positive teamwork habits between the trades.

Successful electrical contractors provide an incentive plan or reward system to encourage field labor to attempt to complete the project within the labor budget. The incentive plan can be paid time off, or perhaps a bonus, based on the number of hours saved compared to the budgeted hours.

Author's Comment: NECAnet.org has a research report entitled *Field Incentive Systems for Electrical Construction.*

Notes

17. Weather/Temperature

Labor units are based on environmental (weather) conditions, which do not reduce labor productivity. Optimum labor efficiency is achieved when the working temperature is between 35°F and 80°F with a relative humidity below 50 percent. Studies have shown that extreme temperatures cause workers to concentrate on their discomfort rather than on the job to be performed, with an increase in accidents, deterioration in workmanship, and lower labor productivity.

Cold. Extremely cold conditions cause a significant reduction in labor productivity because of the need for frequent warm-up breaks. Working in extremely cold environments is very uncomfortable and it often leads to head colds or a feeling of being run-down.

Heat. Elevated temperatures cause a decrease in labor productivity due to the time required to wipe body perspiration from one's face and hands, and from perspiration getting on work surfaces making it difficult to handle material, equipment, and tools. When the temperature is elevated, electricians become fatigued, belligerent, and irritable (let's not go there). They also suffer from diminished powers of concentration under these conditions.

Author's Comment: NECAnet.org has a report available entitled *The Effect of Temperature on Productivity.*

3.11 Are You for Real?

You might be wondering, "If I adjust my labor units to account for these variable factors, how will I ever get a job?" Let's get real, if you choose not to apply any of these labor-unit adjustments for fear that your price will be too high, and you get the job, you will really be in trouble. Better to not get a job that is priced correctly than to get a job and just break even, or worse yet, lose money.

CHAPTER 3

Summary

Notes

Introduction

When you do an electrical estimate, two of the major cost components of the job you will need to determine include material/equipment and labor. The labor component is where the estimate is most likely to go wrong, and where errors can do the greatest damage to the project.

To estimate labor requirements, you start with standard labor-unit guides that tell you how many labor hours it should take to do a certain task under "typical" job conditions.

3.1 What Is a Labor Unit?

A labor unit represents the approximate amount of time required to install an electrical product, component, or piece of equipment. Labor units are based on the assumption that a highly trained, skilled, and motivated electrician is completing the task under a "specific" set of installation conditions, with proper tools and supervision.

3.2 How Labor Units Are Expressed

Labor units are expressed in units of decimal hours so that the hours can be added in a manner similar to dollars and cents, rather than having to add hours and minutes individually.

3.3 Using Work Experience

Electrical work experience is important when you estimate electrical wiring, but you must know when and how to use that experience. There are other factors that should also be taken into consideration, such as supervision, job layout, the handling of tools and material, nonproductive time, and variable job conditions.

3.4 What Is Included in the Labor Unit?

A labor unit has six major components:

- Installation
- Job layout
- Material handling and cleanup
- Nonproductive labor

- Supervision
- Tool handling

Notes

3.5 Labor Units Do Not Include

Labor units do not include the assembly of fixtures or equipment supplied by others. Other factors that are not included in a labor unit are:

- Cutting holes or openings
- Excavation, drilling, or blasting
- Heavy equipment operators' time
- Hoisting material and equipment above three floors
- Maintenance of temporary equipment
- Painting of conduits
- Patching or painting
- Testing or welding
- Sealing fire-rated penetrations

3.6 Labor-Unit Manuals

You must purchase a comprehensive labor-unit manual that contains at least 10,000 labor units. There is no perfect set of labor units that can be applied to all jobs by all electrical contractors. With experience and historical data, you will develop techniques to help you adjust the labor units so they represent your productivity under specific job conditions.

3.7 How to Develop Your Own Labor Units

You will really not develop your own labor units, what you will develop is the "labor-unit adjustment" you will apply to adjust the labor units you are using. To determine your "labor-unit adjustment," compare the estimated hours of a job against the actual number of hours it took.

3.8 Your Labor Units as Compared to Your Competitors

Productivity in the installation of electrical equipment is affected by many factors, and the most significant is project management. If the actual labor exceeds the estimate, the primary cause is usually a deficiency in project management. This is because management determines the labor budget, the level of supervision, and whether the labor force is skilled and motivated enough to be sufficiently productive. Management is also responsible for having the proper tools and material on the job at the right time.

Notes

3.9 Knowing Your Competitors' Labor Units

It does not help you to know the labor units your competitors use because your style of management, your organizational strengths and weaknesses, and the skill of your labor force are all unique to your company.

3.10 Variables That Affect Labor Units

Data from a labor-unit manual must be adjusted to fit the job conditions that you are dealing with. Some job variables can be controlled, whereas others must be accepted as a cost of doing business. You will need to consider some (if not all) of the following factors when adjusting labor units for job conditions.

- Building Conditions
- Change Orders
- Contractor Management Skill
- Embedded and Exposed Wiring
- Job Factors
- Labor Skill
- Ladder and Scaffold Work
- Management
- Material
- Overtime
- Remodel (Old Work)
- Repetitive Factor
- Restrictive Working Conditions
- Schedule
- Shift Work
- Teamwork
- Weather/Temperature

CHAPTER 3

Conclusion

Notes

The ability to determine how many labor hours a job will require is the hardest and most important part of developing an estimate.

You now know what a labor unit is, what is included in one, and equally important, what is not included in a labor unit. You also know how variables can effect labor-unit computations and how to deal with those variables so you end up with an accurate estimate.

Remember to track the amount of labor needed to actually complete each job to ensure the accuracy of the labor-unit adjustments you used. If there is a difference, follow up and find out what happened. Was the job managed properly? Did material prices suddenly increase substantially? Did unexpected conditions cause you to accelerate the job schedule? Did you forget to take something into consideration during the preparation of the estimate? Knowing the answers to questions such as these will help you fine-tune your labor-unit adjustments, and increase your estimating expertise.

Perhaps the most important thing to understand from this chapter is that you will never find a "one size fits all" set of labor-unit data. Next, we will walk you through the first part of the estimating process.

CHAPTER 3

Essay Questions

Notes

1. When you do an electrical estimate, what are two of the major cost components of the job that must be determined?

2. What does a labor unit represent?

3. How are labor units expressed and why?

4. Besides work experience, what other factors should be taken into consideration when completing an estimate?

5. What are the six components of a labor unit?

6. What is not included in a labor unit?

7. How will you develop techniques to help you adjust labor units from labor-unit manuals to represent your productivity under specific job conditions?

8. How do you determine your own labor-unit adjustments?

9. What is the most significant factor that affects productivity in the installation of electrical equipment?

10. Why does it not help for you to know what labor units your competitors use?

11. What variables affect labor units?

Notes

CHAPTER 3

Multiple-Choice Questions

Notes

3.1 What Is a Labor Unit?

1. A labor unit represents the approximate amount of time required to install an electrical product, component, or piece of equipment.

   (a) True
   (b) False

2. The construction and work schedule for a typical project assumes a standard workday, 40 hours per workweek, daylight shift, time to eliminate scheduled overtime, with no more than ______ qualified electricians on the job.

   (a) 25
   (b) 50
   (c) 75
   (d) 100

3. The systems for a typical project assume electrical service by the utility, new listed material, and not more than ______ feet above a solid floor.

   (a) 10
   (b) 15
   (c) 20
   (d) 25

4. The site conditions for a typical project include ______.

   (a) adequate security for material and tool storage
   (b) all new material and new construction
   (c) few interruptions or delays
   (d) all of these

Notes

5. The site conditions for a typical project assume a minimum temperature of _____, a maximum temperature of _____, and 50 percent relative humidity.

(a) 30°F, 83°F
(b) 35°F, 88°F
(c) 40°F, 93°F
(d) 45°F, 95°F

3.2 How Labor Units Are Expressed

6. Labor units are expressed in units of _____ hours.

(a) decimal
(b) hexadecimal
(c) binary
(d) none of these

3.3 Using Work Experience

7. Work experience is important, as a matter of fact it is critical, so it should be your basis for estimating a job.

(a) True
(b) False

3.4 What Is Included in the Labor Unit?

8. A labor unit has six major components.

(a) True
(b) False

9. The actual installation time only represents about _____ percent of the labor unit.

(a) 20
(b) 30
(c) 40
(d) 50

Notes

10. The layout of the work represents _____ percent of the labor unit.

(a) 5
(b) 10
(c) 15
(d) 20

11. Material handling and cleanup represents _____ percent of the labor unit.

(a) 5
(b) 10
(c) 15
(d) 20

12. All jobs include nonproductive labor, which should be managed so as not to exceed _____ percent of the labor unit.

(a) 5
(b) 10
(c) 15
(d) 20

13. Supervision represents _____ percent of the labor unit.

(a) 10
(b) 20
(c) 30
(d) 40

14. The management, handling, and layout of tools represent _____ percent of the labor unit.

(a) 5
(b) 10
(c) 15
(d) 20

Notes

3.5 Labor Units Do Not Include

15. Labor units do not include ______.

(a) the assembly of fixtures
(b) equipment supplied by others
(c) a or b
(d) none of these

3.6 Labor-Unit Manuals

16. You must purchase a comprehensive labor-unit manual that contains at least _____ labor units.

(a) 5,000
(b) 10,000
(c) 15,000
(d) 20,000

3.7 How to Develop Your Own Labor Units

17. You will really not develop your own labor units, what you will develop is the "labor unit ______."

(a) condition
(b) quantifier
(c) average
(d) adjustment

3.8 Your Labor Units as Compared to Your Competitors

18. Productivity in the installation of electrical equipment is affected by many factors, and the most significant is _____.

(a) project management
(b) proper tools
(c) highly trained, skilled, and motivated electricians
(d) coordination of the trades

Notes

19. Labor units are based on the assumption that _____ electricians are completing the task.

(a) highly trained
(b) skilled
(c) motivated
(d) all of these

20. To complete a project efficiently, you must have the material and tools, and all pertinent information, on the job _____.

(a) at all times
(b) when they are needed
(c) only when they are available
(d) none of these

3.9 Knowing Your Competitors' Labor Units

21. It does not help you to know the labor units your competitors use because _____ is(are) unique to your company.

(a) your style of management
(b) your organizational strengths and weaknesses
(c) the skill of your labor force
(d) all of these

3.10 Variables That Affect Labor Units

22. Add _____ percent for the single floor level you are working on. For example, if you are doing a build-out on the ninth floor, increase your total labor by _____ percent.

(a) 1, 9
(b) 1.50, 13.50
(c) 2, 18
(d) 2.50, 22.50

23. Adjust the total building labor hours for buildings with repetitive floor drawings by a factor of ______ percent when there are 15 to 19 floors.

    (a) 2
    (b) 5
    (c) 7
    (d) 13

24. Consider applying a labor adjustment of ______ percent for boxes and ______ percent for raceways when that portion of the wiring method will be exposed

    (a) 1, 5
    (b) 5, 15
    (c) 7, 18
    (d) 10, 20

25. Labor-unit adjustments for ladder work should be considered for any portion of the job that is not at grade level, such as ______ percent when working 12 ft above grade.

    (a) 3
    (b) 5
    (c) 8
    (d) 10

26. Overtime interrupts established life patterns and causes fatigue, reduced motivation, and lower productivity. Consider adjusting all labor hours by ______ percent when your labor force must work six 10-hour days.

    (a) 16
    (b) 17
    (c) 18
    (d) 30

Notes

Notes

CHAPTER 4

THE ESTIMATING PROCESS

INTRODUCTION

Estimating is partly a science and partly an art form. To produce an accurate estimate, you have to collect data, work with many details, and crunch numbers (a science), but you will need to exercise judgment (an art), and doing so may contradict the "science."

Be open to your impressions and feelings; you have them for a reason. If something about the job plays around the edge of your mind and does not seem quite right, look into it. Do not be blinded by the amount of money involved. Your goal is not to overcome "that bad gut feeling," but to find out why it is there.

Companies do not bid on jobs to get work or revenue; they do so to make a profit and to maintain cash flow. If a job does not meet your normal profit targets, you may be better off turning it down. If it will create cash-flow problems, you will have to determine if you can handle those problems, and if doing so is worth the profit you will make on the job. Every business transaction has risk, which is the justification for profits. To be successful you must evaluate and control the risk.

Nail down exactly what the job is going to consist of, and do not take one on that you are not confident you can do in a timely and competent manner. When you see the dollar signs, you may be tempted to take on a job that you are not actually capable of doing. Resist the temptation so you can preserve your reputation and your assets.

You cannot complete a reliable estimate without a drawing and specifications review, so in this chapter we will explain what that means, and then we will explain how to do a take-off to develop the bill-of-material so that you can ultimately determine the cost of the job.

To bid a job, there is a sequence of steps you must complete before you can do the next. If any step is completed incorrectly (or skipped) the subsequent steps will be wrong. If you hurry through one step to get to the next, the results will be unreliable and you will have wasted all of your estimating time.

Notes

4.1 Job Selection

Pre-Bid Checklist

Because there is always a limit to your energy, time, and money, you cannot estimate all jobs that are presented to you. So before estimating any job, ask yourself a few questions:

- Am I qualified to estimate this project?
- Are the contractor and/or owner's scheduling expectations realistic?
- Can I make money on this job?
- Can I manage this job so that it is profitable?
- Do I have enough time to properly estimate this job?
- Do I have the financial resources for this job?
- Do I have the proper tools and equipment to complete this job with profit?
- Do I have the workforce to handle this job?
- Do I want the job?
- Do I want to work with this person or organization?
- Do we have the skills to do this job effectively?
- What is the likelihood of winning the job if my price is competitive?
- What risk does this job present for our company?
- What does my gut say about this project or the contractor and/or owner?
- Will I be competitive?

You do not have to bid every job that is offered, just bid the ones that you believe you have a chance of winning while maintaining a profit margin that meets your needs.

Just Say No!

If you have decided that you are not interested in bidding a given job, immediately communicate this to the appropriate individual and remain firm in your decision. When you decline to bid a job, consider giving the potential customer a competitor's telephone number. You will accomplish two things by this action: you will not waste your time, and you will keep your competitors busy with work you do not want.

Basically, it comes down to the reason an electrical contractor is in business, and that is to make as much money as possible while providing a valued service to your customer. You do not have to bid every job offered, just bid the ones that you believe you have a chance of winning while maintaining a profit margin that meets your needs.

Notes

Financial Resources

Only bid jobs where the anticipated cash flow (you might not get paid on time) provides the funds you need for payroll, material, and overhead. Do not become too excited about the job; you have worked too hard to get where you are to lose it all because the other party either did not pay you on time, or didn't pay you at all. Consider the financial effect of any job before you bid it. If you cannot financially manage it, then do not bid the job.

Many contractors ignore this advice. If you are not convinced, make an appointment with an officer at your bank to discuss general business and financial management. Be sure to ask, "What is the number one reason a business fails?" The answer will be, "Failure to manage cash flow." If you do see a cash-flow crunch coming, talk to your banker before you need the money.

Listen to Your Gut Feelings

You cannot always prove that something is wrong. However, proof is not always necessary to know that you should not take a certain job. For example:

- The customer has an unrealistic completion date. Many contractors bid on such jobs, thinking "we will make it work" (ignore the risk). What happens instead is the job becomes a money-losing fiasco.
- The jobsite gives you the willies. The place is cluttered, and workers do not wear any Personal Protective Equipment (PPE). Do you really want your crew out there?
- The customer insists on a design that contains several *Code* violations. Either the design has not been properly reviewed, or the customer is trying to get away with something. You know you cannot bid on the job as is. When you mention the errors, the customer does not seem concerned.

If you get a bad feeling in your gut when you are in communication with a potential customer, it is a sign that something is not right. Do not allow greed to override that feeling in your gut. Make it a practice to only work for customers you like and who respect you and your staff.

Before you expend any energy estimating a job, do some research on the individual or company; run a credit check and talk with other trades about their reputation for paying bills in a timely manner. Ask who did their electrical work in the past and try to determine why he or she wants to make a change.

There is nothing wrong with telling a potential customer, "We do not wish to bid on this job." If you refuse to bid, you do not have to give a reason even if they ask. It is not your place to teach them to be civil, to have a safe working environment, to behave ethically, or to correct

Notes

whatever problem they have. If they insist on a reason, just tell them there is not a good match between their needs and your company. Do not worry that you will be passing up potential income; you might just be passing up a probable loss.

Many electricians feel obligated to bid a job, even when it is not likely to be profitable. If you do not think you are going to make money on the job, do not bid on it. Remember why you are in business, and that it is better to be honest and up-front than to make excuses or pretend to be interested when you are not. Bidding on jobs you cannot win or on which you cannot make a profit just increases your overhead and will make you less competitive in the future.

4.2 Understanding the Scope of Work

Okay you have decided to bid the job, but before you begin, learn everything you can about the scope of the work to be completed according to the complete set of drawings and specifications.

Plans (Working Drawings)

Be sure that you receive all of the pages of the drawings. Review all notes on other trade drawings for items that may have an impact on the electrical work. These include architectural floor and ceiling drawings, architectural elevation drawings, mechanical drawings, and structural drawings. The first thing to do when you receive them is to make sure they are legible and clear; then verify that you have a full set.

Specifications

Written specifications are additional requirements that govern the material to be used and the work to be performed. Specifications are designed to simplify the task of interpreting the drawings. They should clear up many issues, but they can also add to (or conflict with) the drawings. Some items such as earthwork are covered in other parts of the specifications, such as Section 2. Be sure to review all sections of the project for work that may be assigned to the electrical contractor. Specifications are a part of the "contract bidding documents" and must be considered in your bids. Construction project specifications are typically organized by divisions. There are two different division systems currently in use. You may see either one in projects on which you work.

Traditional System. Specification divisions are defined by a group called The Construction Specification Institute (CSI). The traditional system, which began in 1964, is still used for many projects today.

Notes

Division 16 pertains to most of an electrical contractor's work. It covers both power wiring and equipment, and low-voltage communications systems such as telephone, cable TV, and computer networks. Sometimes a Division 17 is used for low-voltage communications systems. Fire alarm equipment and wiring is usually in Division 13.

New System. In 2004, CSI published an expanded division system, which is becoming increasingly common, so you need to be familiar with it as well. This new system for construction specifications has a total of 49 divisions, where some of them are blank and reserved for future expansion. There are five electrical divisions:

New Specification Divisions (CSI)	
Division 25	Integrated Automation
Division 26	Electrical
Division 27	Communications
Division 28	Electronic Safety & Security
Division 48	Electrical Power Generation

Author's Comment: For the past few years, despite the huge advances in engineering and drafting software, the quality of drawings and specifications has deteriorated significantly. Poor drawings and specifications often result in confusion and an increase in the time it takes to complete the estimate and job. Keep track of all bid inconsistencies and be sure your contract is clear as to what your price reflects.

Visit the Jobsite

Be sure to visit the jobsite before you bid the job. Some electrical contractors use a video and/or digital camera to document the jobsite conditions in an effort to reduce errors with the estimate and prove their visit to the site. This is especially important when doing remodel work as the pictures will remind you of details you may have forgotten. At the very least, be sure to write down what you discover during your site visit.

4.3 Preparing for the Estimate

You need to create a job folder in which to put your bid notes, job information sheet, take-off worksheets, bill-of-material worksheets, quote sheets, summary sheet, and other papers associated with the estimate. This folder can either be of the traditional paper type, or it can be an electronic one.

Notes

Estimate Record Worksheet. This form contains pertinent job information, such as job name, job location and address, telephone numbers, names of the owner, general contractor, architect, engineer, and to whom the bid is to be submitted. This worksheet can be created manually or through estimating software.

Once you have completed the Estimate Record Worksheet, keep it handy for future reference (for example, hang a paper one up on the wall or create a desktop shortcut for an electronic one). This information will be useful when creating a bid proposal.

Estimate Record Worksheet		
Estimate Job Number:	Date:	
Contractor:	Contact	
Address:	City:	State:
Office Phone:	Cell Phone:	
E-mail:	Other:	
Owner:	Contact:	
Address:	City:	State:
Office Phone:	Cell Phone:	
E-mail:	Other:	
Job Name:	Bid Due Date:	
Job Address:	City:	State
Plans and Specifications:		
Date of Plans:	Number of Drawing Pages:	
Architect:	Phone:	E-mail:
Engineer:	Phone:	E-mail:
Telephone:	Phone:	E-mail:
Electric:	Phone:	E-mail:
Electrical Inspector:	Phone:	E-mail:
Other:		
Other:		
Other:		
Notes:		

Notes

4.4 Plans and Specifications Review

Before proceeding any further, carefully read the specifications document and all notes on the drawings so that you have a clear understanding of the scope of the project and the bid requirements before you begin the actual take-off. Remember to take alternates and allowances into consideration, along with knowing whether you are bidding an entire project or simply a piece of a larger one.

If the owner is supplying material, remember to deduct only the material cost of the item(s) supplied. You will still incur costs of handling, storing, labor for any warranty, and all of the other overhead costs and risk factors associated with that material.

Plans

Take a close look at all drawing legends, details, notations, and symbols. Watch for the electrical requirements for control wiring, underground wiring, area lighting, signs, and outdoor equipment. Become familiar with the entire installation and check for any special or unusual features such as elevated ceilings. Check to see if proper working space is provided for the electrical equipment, look for the locations of utilities, and so on.

Case Study No. 1: *A friend of mine, who was just getting started in business, did not read the note on the drawing that required him to replace 180 ft of 4/0 AWG service conductors with 500 kcmil service conductors.*

He underbid the job by $4,000 on a $35,000 job, and he won the job!

Case Study No. 2: *The drawings indicated that the electrical contractor was required to install three of the owner's fixtures. The contractor figured 3 hours for each fixture.*

The actual fixtures weighed over 500 lb each and required three men three days to install!

Specifications

Underline, circle, or highlight important and/or unusual items that can affect the estimate. Some estimators will circle these items before doing the take-off, and only highlight them after taking care of the item in the estimate. Determine who is responsible for painting exposed conduits, trenching, backfill, concrete work, patching, cleanup, temporary power, and so on. Find out if the use of special equipment or overtime is required. Do not take anything for granted.

Notes

Case Study No. 1: According to the specifications a contractor was required to provide a video projector. He guessed that it would cost $5,000.

The result? It actually cost $18,000!

Specifications Checklist

To help you keep track of the drawings and specifications details, complete the Specifications Checklist worksheet as you proceed through the estimate. You will need this information at different stages of the process. Make pertinent notes such as scope and wiring methods for reference as you complete the various steps of the estimate. Create a checklist of important items to be checked off when the estimate is near completion.

Specifications Checklist		
Labor-Unit Adjustment		
1.	Building Conditions	
2.	Change Orders	
3.	Concealed and Exposed Wiring	
4.	Construction Schedule	
5.	Job Factors	
6.	Labor Skill (Efficiency)	
7.	Ladder and Scaffold	
8.	Management	
9.	Material	
10.	Off Hours and Occupied	
11.	Overtime	
12.	Remodel (Old Work)	
13.	Repetitive Factor	
14.	Restrictive Working Conditions	
15.	Shift Work	
16.	Teamwork	
17.	Temperature	
18.	Weather and Humidity	
Labor Adjustment		

Notes

Specifications Checklist (continued)		
Additional Labor		
1.	As-Built Plans	
2.	Demolition	
3.	Energized Parts	
4.	Environmental Hazards	
5.	Excavation, Trenching, and Backfill	
6.	Fire Seals	
7.	Job Location	
8.	Match-Up of Existing Equipment	
9.	Miscellaneous Material Items	
10.	Mobilization (Start-up)	
11.	Nonproductive Labor	
12.	OSHA Compliance	
13.	Plans and Specifications	
14.	Public Safety	
15.	Security	
16.	Shop Time	
17.	Site Conditions	
18.	Subcontract Supervision	
19.	Temporary and/or Standby Power	
Hour Adder		

Notes

Specifications Checklist (continued)		
Direct Job Expenses		
1.	As-Built Plans	$
2.	Business and Occupational Fees	$
3.	Engineering Drawings	$
4.	Equipment Rental	$
5.	Field Office Expenses	$
6.	Fire Seals	$
7.	Warranty	$
8.	Insurance—Special	$
9.	Miscellaneous	$
10.	Mobilization	$
11.	OSHA Compliance	$
12.	Out-of-Town Expenses	$
13.	Parking Fees	$
14.	Permits/Inspection Fees	$
15.	Public Safety	$
16.	Recycle Fees	$
17.	Storage and Handling	$
18.	Subcontract: ________________	$
19.	Supervision Cost	$
20.	Temporary Wiring:	$
21.	Lighting	$
22.	Power	$
23.	Maintenance	$
24.	Testing	$
25.	Trash	$
26.	Utility Cost	$
Total Direct Cost		**$**

Notes

Specifications Checklist (continued)		
Other Final Costs		
1.	Allowances/Contingency	$
2.	Back-Charges	$
3.	Bond	$
4.	Completion Penalty	$
5.	Finance Cost	$
6.	Gross Receipts or Net Profit Tax	$
7.	Inspection Problems	$
8.	Retainage	$
Total Other Cost		**$**
Other Considerations		
1.	Conductor Size—Minimum?	
2.	Raceway Size—Minimum?	
3.	Control Wiring Responsibility?	
4.	Cutting Responsibility?	
5.	Demolition Responsibility?	
6.	Excavation/Backfill Responsibility?	
7.	Painting Responsibility?	
8.	Patching Responsibility?	
9.	Special Equipment?	
10.	Specification Grade Devices or Fittings?	

4.5 Estimate and Bid Notes

If you do not understand something in the drawings or specifications, you might have the tendency to delay the estimate until the last minute. This will result in the bid not being submitted in a timely manner, or worse yet, bidding the job at the last minute without all of the information you need to ensure that it is correct.

Keep a notepad (or electronic text file) handy and write down any questions you have as you proceed through the estimate. If there is anything that is unclear, get the answer as soon as possible—do not wait until the last minute. Contact the architect or engineer, but be sure you have your questions answered as soon as possible.

Notes

Keep a request for information (RFI) log and include this with your proposal.

Using e-mails instead of the telephone is significantly faster, and they create a documentation trail. If you use the phone, make sure you write down the answer to your question on the notepad (or the electronic file) when you receive it. If you do not receive satisfactory answers to your questions, then you are left with a difficult decision—bid the job and list the exclusions in your proposal, or do not bid the job at all. Follow up the phone call with an e-mail noting key details, "Per our conversation today, the following will be included in my proposal."

4.6 Estimating Forms and Worksheets

To quickly and accurately estimate a job, use proper estimating forms and worksheets to save time, create consistency, and help reduce errors. They also help serve as a reminder of items that are easily omitted or forgotten.

Different types of construction, such as residential, commercial, or industrial lend themselves to different types of estimating forms or worksheets. In addition, different types of forms and worksheets are required for different parts of the estimate. For example, a worksheet used to determine lighting requirements is different than those used for feeders and service equipment.

Author's Comment: You can use a computer to design custom worksheets or order them from places like Minnesota Electrical Association, electricalassociation.com/Forms.

4.7 The Take-Off

General

A take-off is the action of counting symbols and measuring lengths that we will later use to determine the bill-of-material. A proper take-off ensures there will be little need to refer to the drawings or specifications to complete the estimate. To accomplish this, you must follow an orderly, organized, methodical routine that is complete and consistent for each and every job.

Use colored pencils, pens, or highlighters to identify each item that you have taken off. The following table contains a sample of a sequence and color code to use to identify those items taken off. Be sure to note what color you use for each step so you won't forget, or so someone else can pick up where you left off if necessary.

Take-off Color Code		
Step	**Sequence**	**Color**
1	Fixtures	Yellow
2	Switches	Blue
3	Receptacles	Light Green
4	Miscellaneous	Purple
5	Circuit Conductors	Pick a color
6	Separate Circuits	Pink
7	Special Systems	Red
8	Feeders	Brown
9	Transformers	Pick a color
10	Service	Pick a color
11	Other	Pick a color

When you have finished the take-off, your drawings should be a colored representation of the electrical work that needs to be installed. **Figure 4–1**

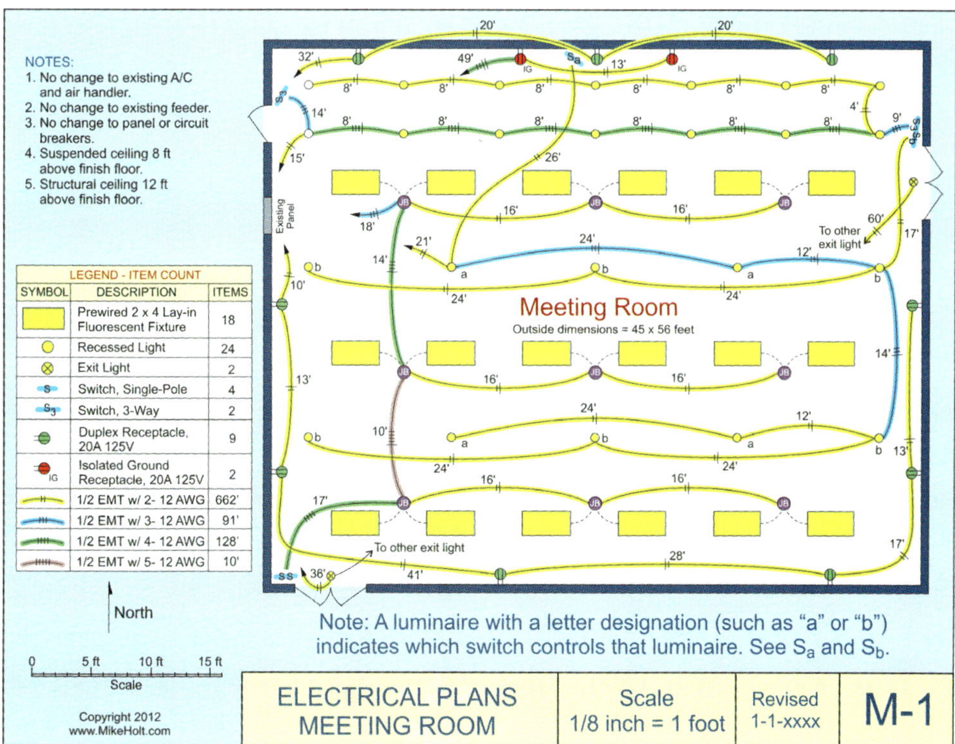

Figure 4–1

Notes

Some people prefer to simply place a check mark on the items they have taken off. Figure 4–2

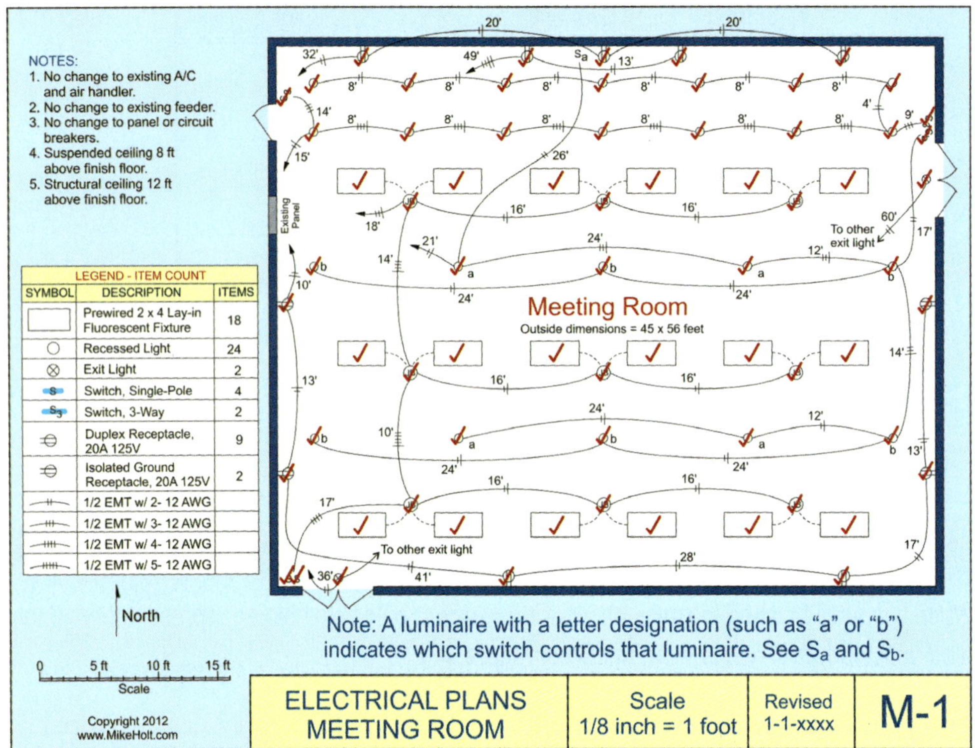

Figure 4–2

If you are not permitted to mark up the paper drawings, then you need to make a full size copy, which can be done at most copy centers. Attempting to estimate a job without color coding the drawings leads to way too many mistakes and errors.

Counting

The purpose of counting symbols is to ascertain and record the quantities of a given electrical component like fixtures, switches, receptacles, and so on, that will be required on the job. This information is used to determine the job's bill-of-material so that we can price the job. To count symbols accurately, you must be capable of reading and interpreting all drawing symbols.

When counting symbols, use a hand-held counter to keep track of the count and after you count a given symbol, mark it with a colored pencil, pen, or highlighter. This ensures that no symbol will be counted more than once, and that no symbol is missed in the take-off. Highlighters are particularly good for marking items since a single motion will color the entire symbol, which can be very helpful when you are checking to see if you have counted all of the items. Figure 4–3

Notes

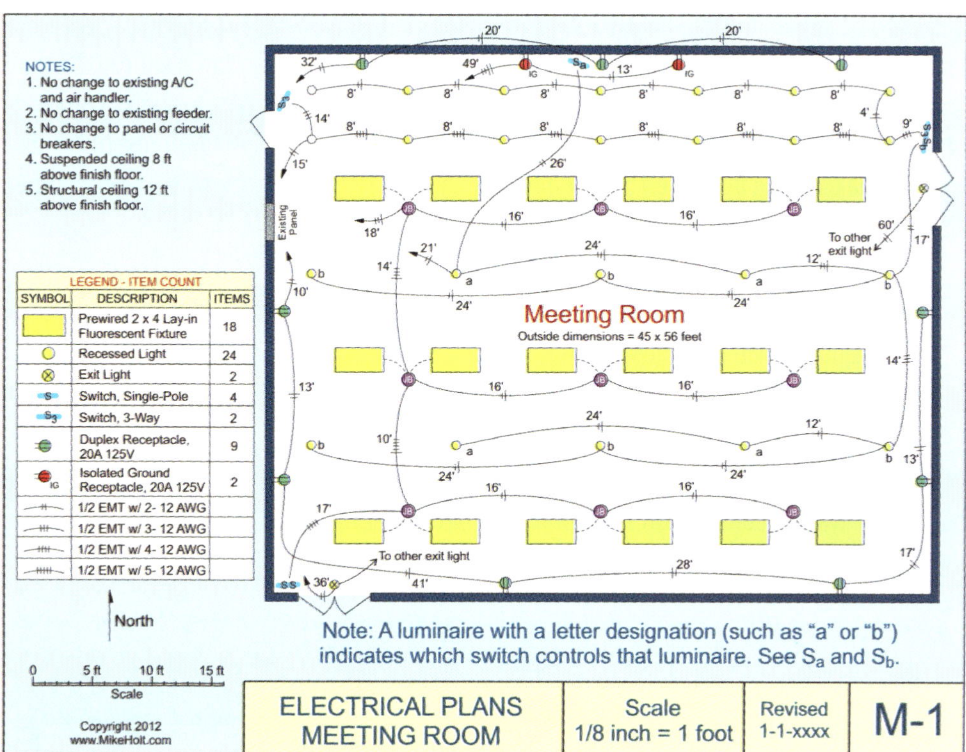

Figure 4–3

Measuring

Measuring consists of determining the circuit length for branch circuits, feeders, and service raceways or cables. Before you begin, verify the architectural scale listed in the drawings especially before measuring any circuit. Test the scale to ensure its accuracy since drawings are sometimes duplicated by a copy center and reduced in size.

Scale dimensions should be noted in the drawing title block; however, the scale might be different on different pages, or different on the same page. If you are not careful, measurements can be off by as much as 100 percent. For example, you might think you are working a ¼ in. per foot scale, and it is actually a ⅛ in. per foot scale.

Tools used to measure the circuits (on a printed drawing) include an architectural ruler, a scaled measuring tape, a mechanical measuring device, or an electronic measuring wheel. The architectural rule is fine for a few quick measurements and verifying the drawing scale, while many estimators use a measuring tape for ⅛ in. and ¼ in. scale drawings. However, the electronic scale wheel is the most convenient since it can easily be set to multiple scales.

Notes

Once you have counted symbols (fixtures, switches, and convenience receptacles), measure the branch-circuit wiring that supplies those openings. When measuring each run, be sure to add in the drops for the overhead circuits for the switches, receptacles, and terminations at panels. Many estimators place a scaled line on the printed drawing to represent the distance of the drops so that when they come across a drop for an outlet or switch opening, they simply measure the distance from the pre-scaled line.

> **Author's Comment:** Electronic scale wheel devices permit you to press one key to add a constant distance to the totals. But if your drops are different lengths, the constant will have to be reset.

When measuring branch circuits, take-off the 2-wire circuits first, the 3-wire circuits next, then the 4-wire circuits. When measuring the circuit wiring, trace the line that represents the wiring with a colored pen or pencil. It does not matter what color you use, just be consistent. **Figure 4–4**

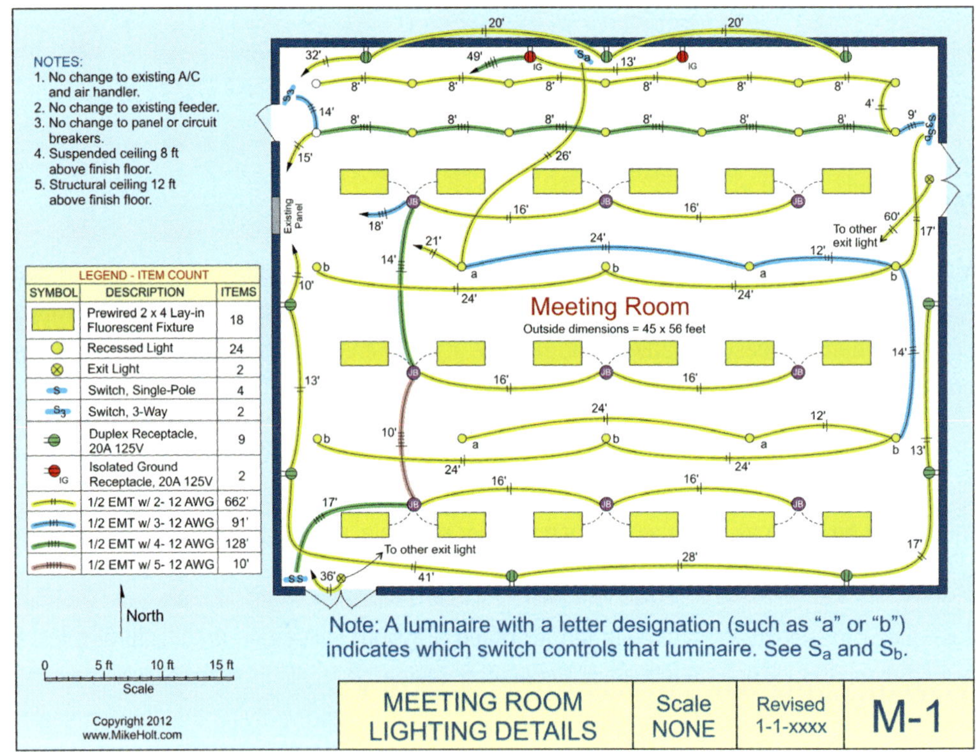

Figure 4–4

> **Author's Comment:** If the drawings do not indicate the circuit layout (most do not), you must perform this task first and then measure the circuit wiring.

Take-Off Sequence

Notes

There is no set sequence for performing the take-off; you will develop a system that fits your personal style and needs. An exception will be those items that require a supplier's quotation since they need time to obtain accurate figures. Whatever system you use, be sure to use the same procedures every time since consistency helps in reducing the time it takes to estimate a job, as well as in reducing errors. The following identifies three typical take-off sequences:

1. Section at a time. Take-off one page of the drawings at a time, or take-off the wiring for the first floor, then all of the wiring for the second floor, and so on.

2. Start at service and end with lighting. Start the take-off at the utility service location, continue taking off the feeders, the branch circuits, and finish by counting the lighting fixtures. This method is time consuming and requires many movements between many pages of drawings and feels unnatural for most people. This style is generally not recommended, but if you have a computer estimating system, it can work out okay.

3. Start with lighting and end with service. This method provides an overview of the job as you count the fixtures, switches, and then the convenience receptacles, which allows you to ease into the estimate. After taking off the homeruns and special circuits, you should have a good idea of the scope of the project and be better prepared to deal with the more complex portions. Lighting fixture suppliers and manufacturers often will not quote unless they have the quantities for each fixture type, so this method can be advantageous when bidding time is short.

When using this take-off sequence, the following order is recommended:

- Count lighting fixtures
- Count switches
- Count receptacles
- Count special systems such as television, telephone, CATV, alarm, security, sound, and so on
- Count motorized and special equipment
- Count panels and service equipment
- Measure feeders and service runs
- Measure wiring for motorized and special equipment
- Measure wiring for special systems such as television, telephone, CATV, alarm, security, sound, and so on
- Measure branch-circuit wiring to outlets and related homeruns
- Measure lighting circuit wiring and related homeruns

Notes

4.8 Determining the Bill-of-Material (Manual Estimate)

Once the take-off is complete, the next step is to determine the bill-of-material, which means determining the type, size, and quantity of all material items required to complete the installation. **Figure 4–5**

LEGEND - ITEM COUNT		
SYMBOL	DESCRIPTION	ITEMS
	Prewired 2 x 4 Lay-in Fluorescent Fixture	18
	Recessed Light	24
	Exit Light	2
S	Switch, Single-Pole	4
S_3	Switch, 3-Way	2
	Duplex Receptacle, 20A 125V	9
IG	Isolated Ground Receptacle, 20A 125V	2
	1/2 EMT w/ 2- 12 AWG	662'
	1/2 EMT w/ 3- 12 AWG	91'
	1/2 EMT w/ 4- 12 AWG	128'
	1/2 EMT w/ 5- 12 AWG	10'

Figure 4–5

If you are estimating manually, determining the bill-of-material requires the estimator to have the ability to visualize all of the material items needed for each symbol. If you do not understand the electrical wiring requirements or do not have that visualization ability, you cannot determine the bill-of-material, which means you really cannot estimate the job properly. **Figures 4–6** and **4–7**

Author's Comment: If you are estimating the job with computer software, the bill-of-material is automatically generated from the take-off. It is still necessary for the estimator to be aware of the components required to be able to verify that the software is generating the correct items.

Notes

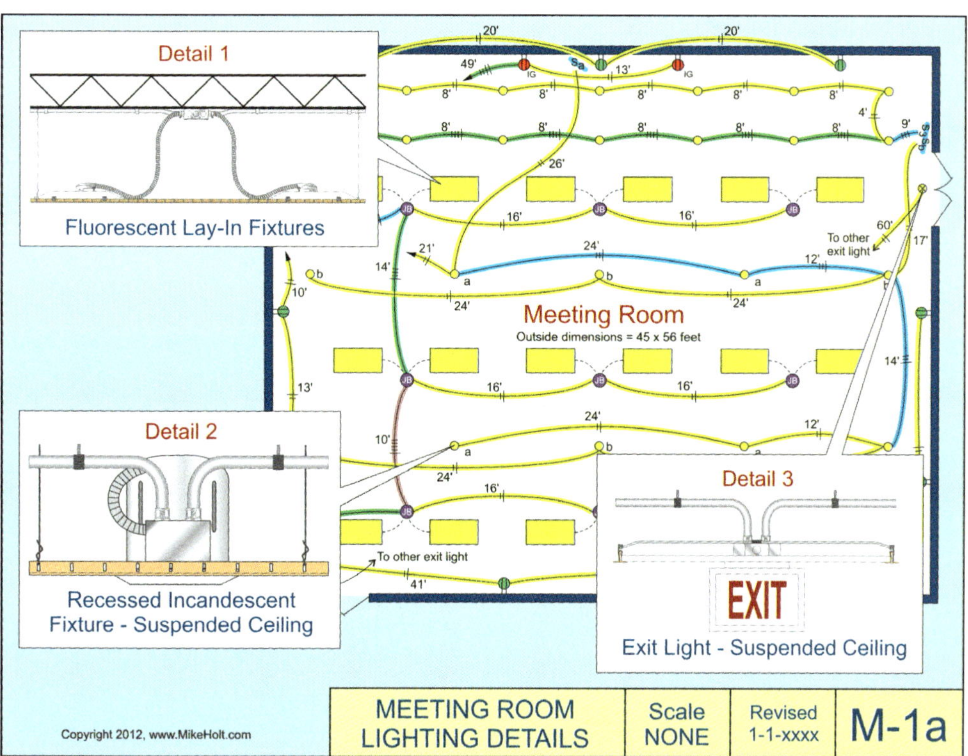

Figure 4–6

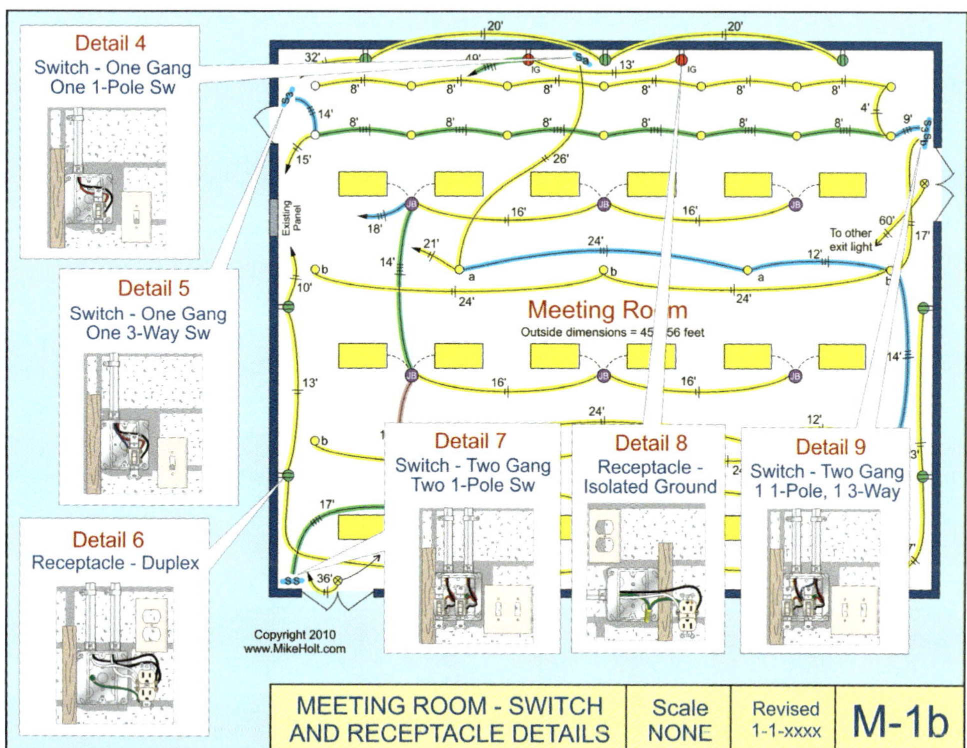

Figure 4–7

Notes

Material Spreadsheet

Manual estimates require the bill-of-material to be extracted from the take-off in the most efficient manner, which is with the use of a spreadsheet.

Author's Comment: The following spreadsheet (Meeting Room Bill-of-Material Spreadsheet) is based on the Meeting Room Drawing. See **Figure 4–1**

Meeting Room Bill-of-Material

		Boxes	½" EMT	Rings			Switches		Switch Plates		Receptacles			Blank
Description	**Qty**	4 x 4"	Conn.	Sq Rd	1 Gang	2 Gang	1-Pole	3-Way	1 Gang	2 Gang	Duplex	Isolated	Plates	Plates
Fixtures														
Fluorescent Lay-in (Detail 1)	18	9	18											9
Recessed (Detail 2)	24		48											
Exit (Detail 3)	2	2	4	2										
Switches														
Switch—Single Pole, 1G (Detail 4)	1	1	2		1		1		1					
Switch—3-Way, 1G (Detail 5)	1	1	2		1			1	1					
Switch—Two 1-Pole, 2G (Detail 6)	1	1	2			1	2			1				
Switch—1-Pole and 3-Way, 2G (Detail 7)	1	1	2			1	1	1		1				
Receptacles														
Receptacle 20A 125V (Detail 8)	9	9	18		9						9		9	
Receptacle IG 20A 125V (Detail 9)	2	2	4		2							2	2	
Totals	**59**	**26**	**100**	**2**	**13**	**2**	**4**	**2**	**2**	**2**	**9**	**2**	**11**	**9**

4.9 Pricing and Laboring

Notes

After developing the bill-of-material, you need to transfer the items and their quantities to the Price/Labor Worksheet for pricing and laboring.

Computer-Assisted Estimates. Pricing and laboring is automatically completed by the computer.

Pricing

The act of pricing consists of looking up the cost for each material item and penciling it onto the Price/Labor Worksheet. To save time, locate the cost for each of the material items before you perform the cost extensions. If you do not have a cost for a particular material item, draw a line through the cost field so that you know later you did not omit it.

Author's Comment: Pay special attention to the unit of measure that the cost reflects, such as "E" for each, "C" for 100, and "M" for 1,000.

Price/Labor (Pricing) Worksheet							
Description	Qty	Cost	U	Ext	Hr	U	Ext
Boxes							
Metal Boxes 4 x 4" Regular	26	$53.70	100				
EMT Set Screw Connectors ½"	100	$13.90	100				
Rings							
Rings, Square Round	2	$75.30	100				
Rings, 1-Gang	13	$43.20	100				
Rings, 2-Gang	2	$10.05	100				
Switches							
Switch - 20A, 125/277V, 1-Pole	4	$348.00	100				
Switch - 20A, 125/277V, 3-Way	2	$355.30	100				
Plates, Plastic 1-Gang Switch	2	$22.40	100				
Plates, Plastic 2-Gang Switch	2	$50.40	100				

Notes

Price/Labor (Pricing) Worksheet (continued)							
Description	Qty	Cost	U	Ext	Hr	U	Ext
Receptacles							
Duplex Receptacle 20A, 125V	9	$188.50	100				
Isolated Ground Receptacle 20A, 120V	2	$1,237.50	100				
Plates, Plastic 1-Gang Duplex Receptacle	11	$22.40	100				
Plate, Raised 4 x 4 Blank	9	$29.90	100				
Raceways							
EMT ½"	891	$15.20	100				
EMT Set Screw Couplings ½" (1 per 10' of EMT)	90	$15.80	100				
Wire							
Wire - 12 THHN, Copper, 600V	2,393	$119.00	1,000				
Fixtures							
Fluorescent Lay-in	18	$58.32	1				
Recessed Light	24	$7.20	1				
Exit Fixture	2	$21.42	1				
Totals				**$0.00**			**0.00**

Laboring

Laboring consists of looking up the labor unit associated with each material item and penciling those values onto the Price/Labor Worksheet. You can save time by locating the labor units for each of the material items before you perform the labor-hour extensions.

Laboring Worksheet							
Description	Qty	Cost	U	Ext	Hr	U	Ext
Boxes							
Metal Boxes 4 x 4" Regular	26	$53.70	100		18.00	100	
EMT Set Screw Connectors ½"	100	$13.90	100		2.00	100	
Rings							
Rings, Square Round	2	$75.30	100		4.50	100	
Rings, 1-Gang	13	$43.20	100		4.50	100	
Rings, 2-Gang	2	$10.05	100		5.00	100	
Switches							
Switch - 20A, 125/277V, 1-pole	4	$348.00	100		20.00	100	
Switch - 20A, 125/277V, 3-Way	2	$355.30	100		25.00	100	
Plate Plastic 1-Gang Switch	2	$22.40	100		2.50	100	
Plates, Plastic 2-Gang Switch	2	$50.40	100		4.00	100	
Receptacles							
Duplex Receptacle 20A, 125V	9	$188.50	100		19.00	100	
Isolated Ground Receptacle 20A, 120V	2	$1,237.50	100		25.00	100	
Plates, Plastic 1-Gang Duplex Receptacle	11	$22.40	100		2.50	100	
Plate, Raised 4 x 4 Blank	9	$29.90	100		6.00	100	
Raceways							
EMT ½"	891	$15.20	100		2.25	100	
EMT Set Screw Couplings ½" (1 per 10' of EMT)	90	$15.80	100		2.00	100	
Wire							
Wire - 12 THHN, Copper, 600V	2,393	$119.00	1,000		4.25	1,000	
Fixtures							
Fluorescent Lay-in	18	$58.32	1		0.75	1	
Recessed Light	24	$7.20	1		1.00	1	
Exit Fixture	2	$21.42	1		0.25	1	
Totals				**$0.00**			**0.00**

Notes

Notes

4.10 Extensions and Totals

After penciling in the material cost and the labor-hour value for each item, you must determine the material cost and labor-hour extensions for them, then calculate the totals for each worksheet page.

Computer-Assisted Estimates. Extending and totaling is automatically completed by the computer.

Material Cost Extension

To determine (or calculate) the material cost extension for each item, divide the material cost by the unit, then multiply that value by the quantity of material items.

> ***Example:*** *The total cost of 26 metal boxes that cost $53.70 per 100 (C) boxes is: $53.70/100 x 26 boxes = $13.96.*

Labor-Hour Extension

Calculate the labor-hour extension for each item by dividing the labor hours by the unit, then multiplying that value by the quantity of the material items.

> ***Example:*** *The total labor to install 26 metal boxes at 18 hours per 100 (C) boxes is: 18.00/100 x 26 boxes = 4.68 hours.*

Important: Have someone else double-check your extensions and totals for each page so you gain confidence that your material cost and labor hours are probably correct. Be certain to double-check owner-supplied equipment and/or material for accurate material and labor pricing.

Notes

Extension and Totals							
Description	Qty	Cost	U	Ext	Hr	U	Ext
Boxes							
Metal Boxes 4 x 4" Regular	26	$53.70	100	$13.96	18.00	100	4.68
EMT Set Screw Connectors ½"	100	$13.90	100	$13.90	2.00	100	2.00
Rings							
Rings, Square Round	2	$75.30	100	$1.51	4.50	100	0.09
Rings, 1-Gang	13	$43.20	100	$5.62	4.50	100	0.59
Rings, 2-Gang	2	$10.05	100	$0.20	5.00	100	0.10
Switches							
Switch - 20A, 125/277V, 1-pole	4	$348.00	100	$13.92	20.00	100	0.80
Switch - 20A, 125/277V, 3-Way	2	$355.30	100	$7.11	25.00	100	0.50
Plate Plastic 1-Gang Switch	2	$22.40	100	$0.45	2.50	100	0.05
Plates, Plastic 2-Gang Switch	2	$50.40	100	$1.01	4.00	100	0.08
Receptacles							
Duplex Receptacle 20A, 125V	9	$188.50	100	$16.97	19.00	100	1.71
Isolated Ground Receptacle 20A, 120V	2	$1,237.50	100	$24.75	25.00	100	0.50
Plates, Plastic 1-Gang Duplex Receptacle	11	$22.40	100	$2.46	2.50	100	0.28
Plate, Raised 4 x 4 Blank	9	$29.90	100	$2.69	6.00	100	0.54
Raceways							
EMT ½"	891	$15.20	100	$135.43	2.25	100	20.05
EMT Set Screw Couplings ½" (1 per 10' of EMT)	90	$15.80	100	$14.22	2.00	100	1.80
Wire							
Wire - 12 THHN, Copper, 600V	2,393	$119.00	1000	$284.77	4.25	1000	10.17
Fixtures							
Fluorescent Lay-in	18	$58.32	1	$1,049.76	0.75	1	13.50
Recessed Light	24	$7.20	1	$172.80	1.00	1	24.00
Exit Fixture	2	$21.42	1	$42.84	0.25	1	0.50
Totals				**$1,804.37**			**81.94**

CHAPTER

4

Summary

Notes

Introduction

Estimating is partly a science and partly an art form. To produce an accurate estimate, you have to collect data, work with many details, and crunch numbers (a science), but you will need to exercise judgment (an art), and doing so may contradict the "science."

You cannot complete a reliable estimate without a drawing and specifications review. To bid a job, there is a sequence of steps you must complete before you can do the next. If you get any step wrong, the subsequent steps will be wrong. If you hurry through one step to get to the next, the results will be unreliable and you will have wasted all of your estimating time.

4.1 Job Selection

Pre-Bid Checklist. Because there is always a limit to your energy, time, and money, you cannot estimate all jobs that are presented to you. So before estimating any job, ask yourself a few questions:

- Am I qualified to estimate this project?
- Are the contractor and/or owner's scheduling expectations realistic?
- Can I make money on this job?
- Can I manage this job so that it is profitable?
- Do I have enough time to properly estimate this job?
- Do I have the financial resources for this job?
- Do I have the proper tools and equipment to complete this job with profit?
- Do I have the workforce to handle this job?
- Do I want the job?
- Do I want to work with this person or organization?
- Do we have the skills to do this job effectively?
- What is the likelihood of winning the job if my price is competitive?
- What risk does this job present for our company?
- What does my gut say about this project or the contractor and/or owner?
- Will I be competitive?

Just Say No! If you have decided that you are not interested in bidding a given job, immediately communicate this to the customer and remain firm in your decision.

Financial Resources. Only bid jobs where the anticipated cash flow (you might not get paid on time) provides the funds you need for payroll, material, and overhead.

Notes

Listen to Your Gut Feelings. You cannot always prove that something is wrong. However, proof is not always necessary to know that you should not take a certain job. Make it a practice to only work for customers you like and who respect you and your staff.

Before you expend any energy estimating a job, do some research on the individual or company; run a credit check and talk with other trades about their reputation for paying bills in a timely manner. Ask who did their electrical work in the past and try to determine why he or she wants to make a change.

4.2 Understanding the Scope of Work

Once you have decided to bid a job, but before you begin, learn everything you can about the scope of the work to be completed according to the complete set of drawings and specifications.

Plans (Working Drawings). Be sure that you receive all of the pages of the drawings. Review all notes on other trade drawings for items that may have an impact on the electrical work, including architectural floor and ceiling drawings, architectural elevation drawings, mechanical drawings, and structural drawings. The first thing to do when you receive them is to make sure they are legible and clear; then verify that you have a full set.

Specifications. Written specifications are additional requirements that govern the material to be used and the work to be performed. Specifications are designed to simplify the task of interpreting the drawings. They should clear up many issues, but they can also add to (or conflict with) the drawings. Be sure to review all sections of the project for work that may be assigned to the electrical contractor. Specifications are a part of the "contract bidding documents" and must be considered in your bids.

Visit the Jobsite. Be sure to visit the jobsite before you bid the job. Some electrical contractors use a video and/or digital camera to document the jobsite conditions in an effort to reduce errors with the estimate and prove their visit to the site. At the very least, be sure to write down what you discover during your site visit.

4.3 Preparing for the Estimate

You need to create a job folder in which to put your bid notes, job information sheet, take-off worksheets, bill-of-material worksheets, quote sheets, summary sheet, and other papers associated with the estimate.

Notes

4.4 Plans and Specifications Review

Carefully read the specifications document and all notes on the drawings so that you have a clear understanding of the scope of the project and the bid requirements before you begin the actual take-off. To help you keep track of the drawings and specifications details, complete the Specifications Checklist worksheet as you proceed through the estimate. Create a checklist of important items to be checked off when the estimate is near completion. Remember to consider alternates, allowances, and owner-supplied material during this process.

4.5 Estimate and Bid Notes

Keep a notepad (or electronic text file) handy and write down any questions you have as you proceed through the estimate. If there is anything that is unclear, get the answer as soon as possible—do not wait until the last minute.

Keep a request for information (RFI) log and include this with your proposal.

Using e-mails instead of the telephone is significantly faster, and they create a documentation trail. If you use the phone, make sure you write down the answer to your question on the notepad (or the electronic file) when you receive it. If you do not receive satisfactory answers to your questions, then you are left with a difficult decision—bid the job and list the exclusions in your proposal, or do not bid the job at all. Follow up the phone call with an e-mail noting key details, "Per our conversation today, the following will be included in my proposal."

4.6 Estimating Forms and Worksheets

To quickly and accurately estimate a job, use proper estimating forms and worksheets to save time, create consistency, and help reduce errors. They also help serve as a reminder of items that are easily omitted or forgotten.

4.7 The Take-Off

A take-off is the action of counting symbols and measuring lengths that we will later use to determine the bill-of-material. A proper take-off ensures there will be little need to refer to the drawings or specifications to complete the estimate. To accomplish this, you must follow an orderly, organized, methodical routine that is complete and consistent for each and every job.

Use colored pencils, pens, or highlighters to identify each item that you have taken off. When you have finished the take-off, your drawings should be a colored representation of the electrical work that needs to be installed. If you are not permitted to mark up the paper drawings, then you need make a full size copy.

Notes

4.8 Determining the Bill-of-Material (Manual Estimate)

Once the take-off is complete, the next step is to determine the bill-of-material, which means determining the type, size, and quantity of all material items required to complete the installation.

Determining the bill-of-material requires the estimator to have the ability to visualize all of the material items needed for each symbol. If you do not understand the electrical wiring requirements or do not have that visualization ability, you cannot determine the bill-of-material.

4.9 Pricing and Laboring

After developing the bill-of-material, you need to transfer the items and their quantities to the Price/Labor Worksheet for pricing and laboring.

4.10 Extensions and Totals

After penciling in the material cost and the labor-hour value for each item, you must determine the material cost and labor-hour extensions for them, then calculate the totals for each worksheet page.

CHAPTER 4

Conclusion

Notes

In this chapter, you saw that preparing an estimate requires performing specific steps in a specific order. You now know the steps and the order in which to perform them.

You cannot do an estimate without developing the bill-of-material, and this chapter showed you how to develop one. We also took you through the subsequent steps, such as pricing material, determining labor hours, and performing material and labor extensions.

Next, we will show you how to determine the break-even cost. This does not mean you are trying to just break even on a job instead of making a profit.

Essay Questions

CHAPTER
4

Notes

1. How is producing an accurate estimate partly a science and partly an art form?

2. What must you do when considering which jobs to bid?

3. What three items are necessary in order to understand the scope of the work to be completed?

4. What is the purpose of the job folder?

5. What is the purpose of the Specifications Checklist?

6. What is the purpose of using a request for information (RFI) log?

Notes

7. What is the purpose of using proper forms and worksheets?

8. What is a take-off and what does a proper take-off ensure?

9. What does determining the bill-of-material mean and what does it require of the estimator?

10. What do you do after the bill-of-material has been developed?

11. What do you do after the pricing and laboring is complete?

CHAPTER 4

Multiple-Choice Questions

Notes

Introduction

1. Companies do not bid on jobs to get work or revenue, they do so to make a profit and to _____.

   (a) keep their employees busy
   (b) maintain cash flow
   (c) stay in tune with the market conditions
   (d) monitor the competition

4.1 Job Selection

2. You should always try to estimate all jobs that are presented to you.

   (a) True
   (b) False

4.2 Understanding the Scope of Work

3. The first thing to do when you receive the drawings is to be sure _____.

   (a) they are legible
   (b) they are clear
   (c) you have a full set
   (d) all of these

4. The traditional system of construction specifications has _____ divisions

   (a) 15
   (b) 16
   (c) 17
   (d) 18

Notes

5. The new system for construction specifications has a total of _____ divisions, where some of them are blank and reserved for future expansion.

(a) 47
(b) 48
(c) 49
(d) 50

4.3 Preparing for the Estimate

6. Once you have completed the Estimate Record Worksheet, _____.

(a) keep it handy for future reference
(b) immediately file it in the job folder
(c) make a copy and send it to the customer
(d) none of these

4.4 Plans and Specifications Review

7. Carefully read the specifications document and all notes on the drawings so that you have a clear understanding of the _____ of the project and the bid requirements before you begin the actual take-off.

(a) location
(b) conditions
(c) scope
(d) all of these

8. Become familiar with the _____ and check for any special or unusual features such as elevated ceilings.

(a) plans
(b) job
(c) specifications
(d) entire installation

Notes

9. Underline, circle, or highlight important and/or unusual items that can affect the _____.

(a) estimate
(b) bid
(c) job
(d) schedule

10. To help you keep track of the drawings and specifications details, complete the _____ as you proceed through the estimate.

(a) Estimate Record worksheet
(b) Specifications Checklist worksheet
(c) bill-of-material
(d) all of these

4.5 Estimate and Bid Notes

11. If there is anything that is unclear, get the answer as soon as possible—do not wait until the last minute. Contact the _____, but be sure you have your questions answered as soon as possible.

(a) general contractor or inspector
(b) customer
(c) architect or engineer
(d) none of these

4.6 Estimating Forms and Worksheets

12. To quickly and accurately estimate a job, use proper estimating forms and worksheets to _____.

(a) save time
(b) create consistency
(c) help reduce errors
(d) all of these

Notes

4.7 The Take-Off

13. A take-off is the action of counting symbols and measuring lengths that we will later use to determine the _____.

(a) estimate
(b) bid
(c) bill-of-material
(d) proposal

14. A proper take-off ensures there will be little need to refer to the drawings or specifications to complete the _____.

(a) estimate
(b) bid
(c) bill-of-material
(d) proposal

15. To count symbols accurately, you must be capable of _____ all drawing symbols.

(a) reading
(b) interpreting
(c) a or b
(d) a and b

16. Measuring consists of determining the circuit length for branch circuits, feeders, and service raceways or cables.

(a) True
(b) False

17. When measuring the circuit wiring, _____ the line that represents the wiring with a colored pen or pencil.

(a) trace
(b) visualize
(c) cross out
(d) dot

Notes

18. The three typical take-off sequences include: section at a time, start at service and end with lighting, or start with lighting and end with service.

(a) True
(b) False

4.8 Determining the Bill-of-Material (Manual Estimate)

19. Once the take-off is complete, the next step is to determine the _____, which means determining the type, size, and quantity of all material items required to complete the installation.

(a) estimate
(b) bill-of-material
(c) labor burden
(d) bid

4.9 Pricing and Laboring

20. If you do not have a cost for a particular material item, _____ so that you know later you did not omit it.

(a) make a note of it on your note pad
(b) do not bid the job
(c) draw a line through the cost field
(d) guess at the cost

21. Laboring consists of looking up the labor unit associated with each material item and penciling those values onto the _____.

(a) Price/Labor Worksheet
(b) Estimate Checklist Worksheet
(c) Bill-of-Material Spreadsheet
(d) Specifications Checklist

Notes

4.10 Extensions and Totals

22. After penciling in the material cost and the labor-hour value for each item, you must determine the material cost and labor-hour extensions for them, then calculate the totals for each worksheet page.

    (a) True
    (b) False

CHAPTER 5 DETERMINING BREAK-EVEN COST

INTRODUCTION

Obviously, nobody wants to just break even on a job. So, why calculate the break-even cost?

Once your bid price covers all of your job costs (the break-even point), every dollar above that is a dollar of profit, but every dollar below it is a dollar of loss. Too many dollars below that cost on too many jobs and your firm goes out of business, as do quite a few electrical contracting companies each year.

In this chapter, you will learn how to determine the component costs of the job and then total them up so you can determine where the break-even point is. This process is not as easy as it might seem, but we will show you a method that is relatively easy and that will make your results consistent and dependable.

It is worth noting that one mistake in this process can be costly. It can even prove fatal to your company. If you are diligent with the method you will learn here, you can avoid that fate.

Throughout the break-even analysis process, you will have to make judgment decisions on intangibles, such as job conditions, labor productivity, material requirements, waste, theft, small tools, direct job expenses, and overhead.

Remember, making a judgment decision does not mean tossing a coin. Making a sound judgment decision requires obtaining whatever relevant information is available, and then logically analyzing the available options.

Do not ever forget that poor judgment can result in a mistake that ruins your company and tarnishes your personal reputation.

Once you understand the methodology for determining the break-even point, you will be able to avoid the related pitfalls that have sunk many electrical contractors. The key to this, however, is your determination to stick to that method and work past the fatigue and frustration that can arise during this process. Do that, and you are likely to consistently have an accurate break-even analysis.

Summarizing the estimate to determine your break-even cost can be overwhelming. One mistake at this point can be costly in terms of loosing a job or worst yet, securing a job at a loss! This part of the estimating process requires you to make judgment calls on job conditions, labor productivity, miscellaneous material requirements, waste, theft, small tools, direct job expenses, and overhead.

Notes

The first step in this process requires you to transfer the totals for labor hours and material costs to the summary worksheet. This document is used to help you organize the different costs so you don't make a mistake. The summary worksheet has seven major sections, and they include:

- Step A—Labor Hours
- Step B—Labor Cost
- Step C—Material Cost
- Step D—Direct Cost
- Step E—Prime Cost
- Step F—Overhead
- Step G—Break-Even Cost

Summary Worksheet		
Labor Cost Summary		
Step A	Labor Hours	81.94
	Adjusted Labor Hours	4.09
	Additional Labor Hours	23.74
	Total Adjusted Labor Hours	109.77
Step B	Labor Cost @$18.00 per hour	$ 1,975.86
Material Cost Summary		
Step C	Material Cost (Price Sheet)	$ 1,804.37
	Miscellaneous Material @ 10%	$ 180.44
	Small Tools @ 3%	$ 54.13
	Waste and Theft @ 5%	$ 90.22
	Taxable Material	$ 2,129.16
	Sales tax @ 7%	$ 149.04
	Total Material Cost	$ 2,278.20
Break-Even Cost		
Step D	Direct Job Costs	$ 550.00
Step E	Prime Costs (A, B, C, and D)	$ 4,804.06
Step F	Overhead	$ 1,975.86
Step G	Break-Even	$ 6,779.92

5.1 Labor Hours (Step A)

The first step in determining your break-even cost is to transfer the labor hours and material cost from the Price/Labor Worksheets to the Estimate Summary Worksheet. The components that make up this worksheet are discussed in the following pages and in Chapter 6. I suggest that you use a spreadsheet to create an Estimate Summary Worksheet that includes the components we discuss so all of your calculations are in one place.

Labor-Unit Adjustments

The estimated labor hours must be adjusted for working conditions based on a percentage of the total (or fixed) man-hours for specific conditions. Determining labor adjustments comes with experience and is part of what makes estimating an art form. With experience from past performances, adjusting labor man-hours for job conditions can be quite accurate; however, at times doing so is simply an educated guess. The following factors must be considered for every job that you estimate. For details on these factors, see Chapter 3, Section 3.10.

Labor-Unit Adjustments [5.1]

Description	Adj.%	Hrs
Estimated Labor Hours		**81.94**
Building Conditions	0%	0
Change Orders	0%	0.00
Embedded and Exposed Wiring	0%	0.00
Construction Schedule	0%	0.00
Job Location	0%	0.00
Labor Skill	0%	0.00
Ladder and Scaffold Work	10%	8.19
Management	0%	0.00
Material	0%	0.00
Remodel (Old Work)	0%	0.00
Repetitive Factor	0%	0.00
Restrictive Working Conditions	0%	0.00
Shift Work	0%	0.00
Teamwork	-5%	-4.10
Temperature	0%	0.00
Labor-Unit Adjustment Hours		**4.09**
Total Labor Hours Including Labor-Unit Adjustments		**86.03**

Notes

Notes

Additional Labor

After you have adjusted the total labor-unit hours, you must consider any additional labor requirements for the job that might apply. Be aware that these conditions are not adjustments of the labor unit for job conditions, but additional labor that might be required, such as:

Additional Labor [5.1]			
Description	**Hr**	**%**	**Hrs**
Total Labor Hours Including Labor-Unit Adjustments			**86.03**
As-Built Drawings			0.00
Demolition	8		8.00
Environmentally Hazardous Material Disposal			0.00
Excavation, Trenching, and Backfill			0.00
Job Location			0.00
Jobsite Meetings	2		2.00
Match-Up of Existing Equipment			0.00
Miscellaneous Material Items		8%	6.88
Mobilization and Demobilization	4		4.00
Nonproductive Labor			0.00
Plans and Specifications			0.00
Power			0.00
Public Safety			0.00
Security			0.00
Service and Warranty	2		2.00
Site Conditions			0.00
Subcontract Supervision			0.00
Training		1%	0.86
Additional Labor Hours			**23.74**
Total Labor Hours Including Additional Labor			**109.77**

As-Built Drawings. As-built drawings are intended to show, in accurate detail, the location of feeders, branch circuits, and the size of equipment. Be sure to include the labor to create and maintain as-built drawings if required by the contract and specifications, or by the building department. Many jobs now require these to be done in an electronic form, by using AutoCAD or a .pdf file format. Some contractors may have the capability to do this in-house, whereas others will need to hire someone to do them.

Author's Comment: Be sure you include the cost for revising as-built drawings when you invoice for change orders.

Notes

Demolition. Some jobs require the removal of the existing electrical wiring and equipment before you begin adding anything new. The labor for demolition must be considered, and again at times it might be just an educated guess. However, with experience you will get a feel as to what factor might be reasonable. You need to verify whether it will be "disconnect and make safe" where others will do the actual removals, or whether you will need to perform the entire disconnecting and removal operations.

Environmentally Hazardous Material. Be sure the bid includes the labor required to handle environmentally hazardous material. This includes preparation, packaging, shipping, and the proper disposal of ballasts, electric-discharge lamps, radioactive exit signs, and so on. Better yet, subcontract it to a company that specializes in that type of work.

Excavation, Trenching, and Backfill. There are places in the country where you cannot plant a bush without a pick. Conversely, if you try to dig a trench in sugar sand on the beach, the more you dig the wider the trench gets, but it does not get any deeper. Poor soil conditions can turn what should be a simple job into a major project. It is often more cost-effective to subcontract this type of work rather than take the entire responsibility of accidentally cutting fiber optic cable, telephone wires, underground high-voltage utility lines, sprinkler and water pipes, or a gas main.

Job Location. If the job is not located in the area of your shop, you need to add travel time. Also consider that it will be more difficult to manage the job and to get the material there when needed. The following example should help you understand how to determine travel time.

Example: *What is the total travel time required for a 212-hour job that has three workers, assuming travel time of 1 hour per worker per day?*

(a) 5.25 hours (b) 8.75 hours (c) 10 hours (d) 30 hours

Answer: *(d) 30 hours*

Job Days = Total Job Hours/Hours Worked per Day
Job Days = 212 hours/21 hours per day (3 workers at 7 hours per day)
Job Days = 10 travel days

Travel time = 1 hour per day per worker x 3 workers x 10 days
Travel time = 30 hours

Notes

Job Meetings. Do not forget to add labor for jobsite safety meetings and other planned meetings of jobsite staff. You might be required to attend meetings even before your phase of the job begins, so be sure to check the plans and specifications carefully.

Match-Up of Existing Equipment. Maybe you have a situation where you are required to match existing equipment, colors, or luminaries. This can become very time consuming and costly so be sure to account for this expense.

Miscellaneous Material Items. It is impractical to try to determine the labor for every material item required for a job. Add 8 percent to the total estimated labor hours for miscellaneous material items not counted or measured when using the manual estimating method.

Computer-Assisted Estimate. There is typically no need to make any labor-hour adjustment for miscellaneous material items, since the software should account for all material required to complete the job.

Mobilization and Demobilization. Do not forget to include the labor required to set up and close down the job, such as preparing the job trailer to be moved.

Nonproductive Labor. Labor units include a prorated amount of the normal nonproductive labor experienced on a typical project. On some projects the nonproductive labor is greater than the normal amount, and the estimated labor for the installation of the electrical systems must be increased accordingly. For example, the owner or general contractor may allow or require all construction crafts to take coffee breaks at a specific time and for a specific duration. The evaluation and determination of the magnitude of abnormal productivity is extremely difficult because there are no standard percentages, mathematical formulas, or guidelines that can be used. The evaluation of the cause and effect of abnormal nonproductive situations can only be determined by the judgment of an experienced person. In estimating the project labor requirements, the electrical contractor must evaluate all the known and anticipated project conditions that will affect the labor productivity and then adjust the estimated labor man-hours accordingly.

A substantially different condition exists when estimating the labor for change orders. You not only must evaluate the magnitude of the nonproductive labor before any change order is received, but the change order itself always increases the nonproductive labor and the supervisory labor to some degree. The issuance of a single typical small change order does increase the nonproductive labor, but usually not in measurable amounts. However, after several change orders are issued, or when a single change order of substantial size is issued, the electrical contractor will always experience a major increase in lost productivity.

Labor units include 5 percent for nonproductive labor. Does this job have the potential for excessive nonproductive time?

Breaks. When you are on a job for a while, your employees get to know those who work with the other trades, and breaks tend to become longer and more frequent if they do not have proper supervision.

Distracting Job Conditions. Is this job going to be directly on a beach, marina, or other areas where the workers will be distracted?

> ***Case Study:*** *In Daytona Beach during "Spring Break" you should increase the labor requirements by some factor for work performed directly on the beach.*

Inspection Tours. Inspection tours are a fact of life and the larger the job, the more frequent and longer the tours. Sometimes projects have multiple inspectors for the different systems, often by different inspection agencies. Do not forget about these!

Plans and Specifications. If adequate drawings and specifications are not provided, add a factor to account for anticipated nonproductive time to figure out what is required. Labor units assume that you have clear and conflict-free drawings and specifications. If this is not the case, inform the general contractor or the owner that your bid includes additional labor as a contingency.

Power. Labor to ensure that temporary, standby, or emergency power is available must be included in the bid if required. Remember to take any need for maintenance into consideration too.

Public Safety. Public safety is a factor, especially when doing work for city, county, state, or federal governmental agencies. Are you required to install traffic cones, barricades, or security gates? Will you be required to have flaggers, or possibly stand-by personnel? Be sure to read the specifications closely and plan your estimate accordingly to account for the labor as well as the cost for safety products.

Security. When working in some governmental and private facilities, you are required to follow specific procedures to receive clearance to enter the premises. Some facilities require that security be notified well in advance of persons desiring entry into the premises and they have to wait for someone to escort them while in the facility. Include monies for badges and drug testing because your personnel might also have to have drug testing done, or attend site specific orientation meetings or courses.

Service and Warranty. No job is installed perfectly, so add some labor to cover service and warranty work.

Notes

Notes

Site Conditions. Because of traffic conditions, projects in the downtown areas of large cities can cause significant lost time. Traffic conditions and narrow streets make it difficult to unload material and equipment. Inadequate parking and storage space are also potential problems. Parking costs in large cities like Chicago can be very expensive, in the range of $25 to $ 50 per day.

Subcontract Supervision. Do not forget to include the labor required for your electricians to supervise and direct subcontractors.

Training. Do you pay your electricians to attend a training and certification program? Include the cost of regular safety training and any required personal protective equipment (PPE) that you provide. It will be wise to add 1 percent to cover labor training.

5.2 Labor Cost (Step B)

The estimated labor cost for a job is determined by multiplying the total adjusted labor man-hours by the labor rate per man-hour.

Labor Cost Example: *The total adjusted estimated labor is 109.77 hours and the labor rate per man-hour is $18.00.*

Estimated labor cost = Total adjusted estimated labor hours x labor rate per man-hour
Estimated labor cost = 109.77 hours x $18.00
Estimated labor cost = $1,975.86

5.3 Labor Rate per Man-Hour

The labor rate per man-hour can be determined by one of two methods: the shop average, or the job average.

Author's Comment: The labor rate per man-hour is significantly different in different parts of the country. In some areas, a journeyman electrician is paid less than $20 per hour, and in other areas, the rate is over $50 per hour.

Shop Average Labor Rate

The shop average labor rate per man-hour is determined by dividing the total field labor cost over a given period of time by the total number of field man-hours over the same period of time.

Shop Average Labor Rate Calculation Example			
Month	Labor Cost	Hours	Rate/Hr
April	$24,000	1,166	$20.58
May	$30,000	1,666	$18.01
June	$36,000	2,167	$16.61
July	$24,000	1,250	$19.20
August	$30,000	1,584	$18.94
September	$36,000	2,167	$16.61
Six Months	**$180,000**	**10,000**	**$18.00**

Notes

Author's Comment: When using the shop average labor rate per man-hour, it might be too low for jobs that require greater skill (such as control wiring), or too high for simple jobs that require less skill (such as residential wiring).

Job Average Labor Rate

Another approach in determining the labor rate per man-hour is to use the anticipated job average labor rate per man-hour. This method requires you to consider how you plan on manning the job; meaning who will be there and what the skill level and wage rate are relative to each other. Review the following example:

Job Average Labor Rate Calculation Example			
Crew	Rate	# of Persons	Extension
Foreman	$25.00	1	$25.00
Journeyman	$20.00	1	$20.00
Apprentice	$15.00	3	$45.00
Total		5	**$90.00**
Weighted Rate-Per-Hour			**$18.00**

Author's Comment: For "prevailing wage" jobs, be sure to use the rate required in the specifications.

Notes

5.4 Labor Burden

In addition to the cost of labor, there are other costs associated with labor that must be taken into consideration. These include employer paid Social Security and Medicare taxes, Workers' Compensation insurance, as well as employee benefits. These costs are identified as "labor burden" costs.

Federal and State Charges. The current Social Security FICA Tax Rate = 7.65 percent; the Social Security Limit = $102,000 (verify amounts for other items) of wages, the Federal Unemployment tax (FUTA) is 0.80 percent of the first $7,000 of wages, the Medicare contribution is 1.45 percent of the total wages, and state unemployment is about 3.50 percent of total wages. We can round this off to about 10 percent.

Workers' Compensation. The percentage is based on total wages paid and it varies from state to state and from contractor to contractor, based on the contractor's number of years in business in the state and claims-related experience. Workers' Compensation, unlike payroll taxes, is applied to total wages, and the cost should be between 7 and 15 percent of the total payroll.

Employee Benefits. Employee benefits might include life, accident and health insurance plans, pension plans, civic and personal leave, severance pay, and vacation and holiday pay. A reasonable number is about 25 percent at a minimum.

Labor burden expenses are generally listed in the income statement under overhead. When this occurs, labor burden will be applied to the estimate when overhead is applied. We will assume that is the case for the purpose of this textbook.

5.5 Total Material Cost (Step C)

The second step in determining your break-even cost is to transfer the material cost from the Price/Labor Worksheets to the Estimate Summary Worksheet. Once this is accomplished, you will need to account for lighting fixtures and switch gear, miscellaneous material, sales tax, small tools, and waste and theft.

Lighting Fixtures

In an attempt to maintain high profit margins, suppliers often hold prices until the last moment before the bid so their competitors will not have a chance to undercut them. You need to have the Estimate Summary Worksheet completed ahead of time. If the quoted items have not been inserted, then a reasonable "guess" must be noted instead. This will avert an omission of high value materials. This way, when the last minute quote prices arrive, you can determine the bid price. Be sure to review the quote when it arrives to ensure substitutions were not made. If they were, you may need to talk to the supplier to ensure you will not have to bear an additional cost if the substitutions are not acceptable.

Notes

> **Author's Comments:** Be careful not to make a mistake when transferring the supplier's prices to the Summary Worksheet. Insist on written quotes, and be sure the quote includes any freight and shipping costs.

Miscellaneous Material

It is impractical to try to determine every material item required for a job, like mounting screws, pulling compound, wire connectors, tape, and so on. You can either try to take them off or add a percentage to the total cost of material as an adjustment; I suggest you add 10 percent of the material cost as a factor when you are doing the estimate manually.

Computer-Assisted Estimate. A 2 to 3 percent adjustment to the total material cost should be sufficient for small items not taken off.

Switchgear Quotes

In an attempt to maintain high profit margins, suppliers often hold prices until the last moment before the bid so their competitors will not have a chance to undercut them. You need to have the Estimate Summary Worksheet completed ahead of time. If the quoted items have not been inserted, then a reasonable "guess" must be noted instead. This will avert an omission of high value materials. This way, when the last minute quote prices arrive, you can determine the bid price.

> **Author's Comment:** Be careful not to make a mistake when transferring the supplier's prices to the Summary Worksheet. Insist on written quotes, and be sure the quote includes any freight and shipping costs.

Notes

Tools

Costs for ladders, cords, cordless drills, screw guns, drill bits, hacksaw blades, and countless other small tools must be included in the estimate. A factor of 3 percent of the total material cost is considered an acceptable value for small tools.

Waste and Theft

In addition, be sensitive to the cost effect of workers wasting material, and to theft on the jobsite. What is a reasonable factor to include for waste or theft? For an organized and efficient organization that manages material carefully, a reasonable factor is 5 percent, but you will not really know unless you do a study to determine this adjustment.

Sales Tax

Sales tax varies from state to state, county to county, and also from city to city. Be sure you are familiar with the sales tax rules in the area where the job is located.

Material Cost Totals		
Description	%	Cost
Estimated Material Cost		**$1,804.37**
Lighting Fixture Quote		$0.00
Miscellaneous Material	10%	$180.44
Small Tools	3%	$54.13
Switch Gear Quote		$0.00
Waste and Theft	5%	$90.22
Taxable Material		$2,129.16
Sales Tax	7%	$149.04
Total Material Cost		**$2,278.20**

Author's Comment: Do not forget to include freight and shipping costs (which are not taxable).

5.6 Direct Job Expenses (Step D)

Notes

Step three in determining the break-even cost is to account for direct job expenses which are often not shown on the drawings, but probably indicated in the specifications.

Direct Job Expenses [5.6]	
Allowance and Contingencies	$0.00
Business and Occupational Fees	$50.00
Coordination Drawings	$0.00
Engineering/Working Drawings	$0.00
Equipment/Rental	$200.00
Job Insurance/Bond	$0.00
OSHA Compliance (Safety Equipment)	$0.00
Out-of-Town Expenses	$0.00
Parking Fees	$0.00
Permits and Inspection Fees	$300.00
Public Safety	$0.00
Recycling Fees	$0.00
Storage	$0.00
Temporary Power	$0.00
Testing and Certification Fees	$0.00
Trash Disposal	$0.00
Utility Charges and Fees	$0.00
Total Direct Job Expenses	**$550.00**

Allowances and Contingencies. If the specifications require an allowance to cover the cost of certain items, be sure your bid includes this.

> **Author's Comment:** You might want to consider a contingency clause to protect you against dramatic cost increases in steel conduit and copper wire prices.

Notes

Business and Occupational Fees. If you need to purchase a business license or pay an occupational fee for the job, be sure your estimate includes this expense.

Coordination Drawings. It is becoming commonplace for the MEP (Mechanical, Electrical, and Plumbing) trades to complete coordination drawings prior to the actual installation, to account for the clashes and collisions in the limited ceiling areas and mechanical rooms for these infrastructure installations. Be certain to account for CAD personnel, coordination meeting time, and drawing reprographics in your estimate.

Engineering/Working Drawings. If you intend to make changes to the job's design, particularly for value-engineered jobs (an alternate means of accomplishing the same end result), you will need to submit revised drawings, so do not forget to include architectural or engineering costs in your estimate.

Equipment/Rental. Remember to include the cost for equipment, trailers, computers, fax and copy machines, radios and cell phones, office personnel, vehicles, and any other such job related expenses.

Job Insurance/Bond. Be careful, the specifications might require you to secure insurance and/or performance bonding. Do not miss this!

OSHA Compliance. Be sure to include OSHA-related products such as safety rails, straps, personal protective equipment (PPE), and ladder tie-downs.

Out-of-Town Expenses. When bidding a job outside your local area, consider travel expenses, tolls, gas, lodging, meals, Internet access, and long-distance telephone calls or cell phones.

Parking Fees. Parking fees for jobs in major cities can be very expensive!

Permits and Inspection Fees. The cost of permits and special inspections can range from a few hundred to many thousands of dollars.

> **Author's Comment:** Where possible, have the owner and/or contractor be responsible for the cost of permits.

Public Safety. Public safety is a factor, especially when doing work for city, county, state, or for federal governmental agencies. Are you required to purchase or rent safety cones, barricades, or security gates? What about security personnel?

Notes

Recycling Fees. Federal and state laws often require the proper disposal of environmentally hazardous products. Watch out for this when disposing of existing electrical products that might contain hazardous chemicals within the product.

Storage. Storage space on the jobsite is often a must, so be sure to include this cost (containers/trailers) in the estimate.

Author's Comment: If the job turns bad, you might not be permitted back on the jobsite to remove your trailer, material, tools, or equipment. If things appear to be going sour, get your trailer and equipment off the job to a safe location as quickly as possible.

Case Study: *I know of a few cases where the owners did not pay the electrical contractors and prevented them from entering the premises to retrieve their material, equipment, and tools. By the time the contractors secured a court order requiring the owner to give access, their equipment and tools were long gone—with the owner claiming no knowledge of their whereabouts!*

Temporary Power. When estimating temporary power, be sure you are clear in your proposal as to what you intend to provide. Do not agree to vague phrases in the contract such as, "Provide temporary power as needed." Be specific in your proposal and indicate the size and voltage of the service, number of poles, lights, receptacles, switches, and any other item that might be required. If your bid does not include maintenance and repairs, or utility connection charges, be sure to say so in your proposal. Sometimes it is more practical to do a take-off of the temporary power during the take-off phase of the estimate.

Case Study: *The contract specified that the electrical contractor would supply all temporary power. He failed to visit the jobsite and assumed a basic temporary pole in the estimate. But later (after winning the bid) he found out that no electric utility power was available within two miles of the job and he was required to supply generators for one year, including the cost of fuel and maintenance.*

Testing and Certification Fees. Do the job specifications require that electrical systems be tested and/or certified in some manner, like meggering the wiring or ground resistance validation?

Trash Disposal. Who covers the cost of trash that has to be removed from the site? If it is thrown in the dumpster, will you be charged a portion of the overall cost by the general contractor? Make sure your contract is clear on this subject.

Utility Charges and Fees. Who is responsible for paying the electric utility service deposit and monthly electric charge?

Notes

5.7 Estimated Prime Cost (Step E)

"Estimated Prime Cost" is simply a term used to identify the subtotaled cost of labor, material, and direct costs. The term allows us to clearly identify the number to which overhead is to be applied. Various electrical estimating software programs may use terms such as "Raw Costs," "Job Subtotal," or simply "Subtotal." Whatever term is used, the function of that term remains the same. Calculating your estimated prime cost is just the simple matter of adding up the labor, material, and direct job costs.

Prime Cost [5.7]		
Labor Cost (Hrs x Rate)	$18.00	$1,975.86
Labor Burden (Included When Overhead is Applied)		$0.00
Material Cost		$2,278.20
Direct Job Cost		$550.00
Prime Cost		**$4,804.06**

5.8 Overhead (Step F)

The cost related to the operation and management of the company, such as rent, insurance, vehicles, administrative salaries, professional fees, and so on, is known as "overhead" and is usually obtained from your income statement or your accountant.

Small Contractor Income Statement Year Ending December 31		
Sales	$250,000	100% of Sales
Direct Job Cost		
Labor (4,000 Hrs)	$80,000	
Material	$70,000	
Total Direct Cost (Prime Cost)	$150,000	60% of Sales
Gross Profit	$100,000	40% of Sales
Overhead Expenses (Administrative Cost)		
Salaries and Commissions	$15,000	
Advertising	$5,000	
Auto and Gas	$10,000	
Benefits	$20,000	
Interest	$1,000	
Insurance—Auto, General, Workman's Comp.	$5,000	
Miscellaneous Expense	$3,000	
Payroll Taxes	$8,000	
Rent	$5,000	
Utilities/Phone	$3,000	
Total Administrative Expenses (50% of Prime)	$75,000	30% of Sales
Net Profit Before Taxes (16.67% of Prime)	**$25,000**	**10% of Sales**

Notes

Notes

Author's Comment: As business volume increases, the cost of overhead per labor hour decreases and smaller jobs and/or smaller size contractors have a higher ratio of overhead cost to labor as compared to larger jobs or larger size contractors.

Medium Contractor Income Statement Year Ending December 31		
Sales	$1,000,000	100% of Sales
Direct Job Cost		
Labor (4,000 Hrs)	$400,000	
Material	$300,000	
Total Direct Cost (Prime Cost)	$700,000	70% of Sales
Gross Profit	$300,000	30% of Sales
Overhead Expenses (Administrative Cost)		
Salaries and Commissions	$60,000	
Advertising	$10,000	
Auto and Gas	$20,000	
Benefits	$80,000	
Interest	$5,000	
Insurance—Auto, General, Workman's Comp.	$25,000	
Miscellaneous Expense	$10,000	
Payroll Taxes	$30,000	
Rent	$5,000	
Utilities/Phone	$5,000	
Total Administrative Expenses (38% of Prime)	$250,000	25% of Sales
Net Profit Before Taxes (7.14% of Prime)	$50,000	5% of Sales

Author's Comment: Overhead application is beyond the scope of most electrical contractors without the assistance of an accountant or bookkeeper, but you need to know it.

5.9 Overhead Calculation Methods

There are two methods of applying overhead to a job: the percentage to prime cost method or the rate per labor-hour method.

Percentage to Prime Cost

Notes

Most contractors apply overhead as a percentage of prime cost. This method has worked well for many contractors over many years, but it is most accurate when applied where the contractor does jobs that are similar in size and content. For example, the percentage to prime cost method of applying overhead works well for a contractor that does strictly residential housing or one that does only office build-outs. This method should not be used by a contractor that does many different types of jobs such as residential, commercial, service, and so on, because the management demands are different for each type of job.

Cost Per Labor Hour

The percentage method is really only suitable when it is being used on similar jobs where the ratio of material cost to labor cost is approximately the same from job to job. Also, one has to be careful to apply the correct multiplier to the prime cost.

Since overhead is related primarily to the management of labor and not the cost of material, it should be applied to the labor man-hours of a job. We can calculate this value by dividing the overhead dollars for a given period of time by the actual field man-hours for the same period of time. Review the following example:

Overhead Cost Per Labor Hour			
Month	Overhead Cost	Labor Hours	Cost Per Hour
April	$25,000	1,166	$21.44
May	$30,000	1,666	$18.01
June	$35,000	2,167	$16.51
July	$25,000	1,250	$20.00
August	$30,000	1,584	$18.94
September	$35,000	2,167	$16.51
Six Months	**$180,000**	**10,000**	**$18.00**

Author's Comment: If you are not sure how to apply overhead to a job using the cost per labor hour, then apply overhead as the same value as your labor cost. Better yet, seek the advice of a good accountant.

Notes

5.10 Break-Even Cost (Estimated Cost) (Step G)

Let's determine our break-even cost or what we estimated it will cost to do the job. All you need to do is add the cost of labor, material, direct job expenses, and overhead together.

Break Even [5.10]		
Labor Cost (109.77 hrs x $18.00/hr)		$1,975.86
Labor Burden (Included When Overhead is Applied)		$0.00
Material Cost		$2,278.20
Direct Job Cost		$550.00
Estimated Prime Cost		$4,804.06
Overhead ($18 per Labor Hour)	$18.00	$1,975.86
Break Even		**$6,779.92**

The argument I hear at this point in my estimating classes is, "If I consider all of these factors and account for them in the estimate, I will never get a job!" But let's slow down and remember what we are trying to accomplish—we are looking to determine our cost (the estimate). Once you know what you think it will cost you to cover all of your job costs (your break-even cost), you are welcome to make any business decision you want, but hopefully you will not sell the job for less than you think it will cost you to complete it—just so you win the job. Remember we have not even added profit yet!

Summary

CHAPTER 5

Notes

Introduction

Once your bid price covers all of your job costs (the break-even point), every dollar above that is a dollar of profit, but every dollar below it is a dollar of loss.

It is worth noting that one mistake in calculating the break-even point can be costly. Throughout the break-even analysis process, you will have to make judgment decisions on intangibles, such as job conditions, labor productivity, material requirements, waste, theft, small tools, direct job expenses, and overhead.

5.1 Labor Hours

The first step in determining your break-even cost is to transfer the labor hours and material cost from the Price/Labor Worksheets to the Estimate Summary Worksheet.

Labor-Unit Adjustments. The estimated labor hours must be adjusted for working conditions based on a percentage of total (or fixed) man-hours for specific conditions. Determining labor adjustments comes with experience and is part of what makes estimating an art form.

Additional Labor. After you have adjusted the total labor-unit hours, you must consider any additional labor requirements for the job that might apply. Be aware that these conditions are not adjustments of the labor unit for job conditions, but additional labor that might be required, such as:

- As-Built Drawings
- Demolition
- Environmentally Hazardous Material Disposal
- Excavation, Trenching, and Backfill
- Job Location
- Jobsite Meetings
- Match-Up of Existing Equipment
- Miscellaneous Material Items
- Mobilization and Demobilization
- Nonproductive Labor
- Plans and Specifications
- Power
- Public Safety
- Security
- Service and Warranty

Notes

- Site Conditions
- Subcontract Supervision
- Training

5.2 Labor Cost

The estimated labor cost for a job is determined by multiplying the total adjusted labor man-hours by the labor rate per man-hour.

5.3 Labor Rate per Man-Hour

The labor rate per man-hour can be determined by one of two methods: the shop average, or the job average.

5.4 Labor Burden

In addition to the cost of labor, there are other costs associated with labor that must be taken into consideration. These include employer paid Social Security and Medicare taxes, Workers' Compensation insurance, as well as employee benefits. These costs are identified as "labor burden" costs.

Labor burden expenses are generally listed in the income statement under overhead. When this occurs, labor burden will be applied to the estimate when overhead is applied.

5.5 Total Material Cost

The second step in determining your break-even cost is to transfer the material cost from the Price/Labor Worksheets to the Estimate Summary Worksheet. Once this is accomplished, you will need to account for lighting fixtures and switch gear, miscellaneous material, sales tax, small tools, and waste and theft.

5.6 Direct Job Expenses

Step three in determining the break-even cost is to account for direct job expenses which are often not shown on the drawings, but probably indicated in the specifications. Direct job costs include:

- Allowances and Contingencies
- Business and Occupational Fees

- Coordination Drawings
- Engineering/Working Drawings
- Equipment/Rental
- Job Insurance/Bond
- OSHA Compliance (Safety Equipment)
- Out-of-Town Expenses
- Parking Fees
- Permits and Inspection Fees
- Public Safety
- Recycling Fees
- Storage
- Temporary Power
- Testing and Certification Fees
- Trash Disposal
- Utility Charges and Fees

Notes

5.7 Estimated Prime Cost

"Estimated Prime Cost" is simply a term used to identify the subtotaled cost of labor, material, and direct costs. The term allows us to clearly identify the number to which overhead is to be applied. Calculating your estimated prime cost is just the simple matter of adding up the labor, material, and direct job costs.

5.8 Overhead

The cost related to the operation and management of the company such as rent, insurance, vehicles, administrative salaries, professional fees, and so on is known as "overhead" and is usually found on your income statement.

5.9 Overhead Calculation Methods

There are two methods of applying overhead to a job: the percentage to prime cost method or the rate per labor-hour method.

5.10 Break-Even Cost (Estimated Cost)

To determine break-even cost all you need to do is add the cost of labor, material, direct job expenses, and overhead together.

CHAPTER 5

Conclusion

Notes

The more accurate your information is about your cost of doing business, the more accurately you will be able to calculate the break-even point for a particular type of job. Knowing the break-even point is vitally important when estimating a job, because this is the point at which you will never lower your price if you expect to make any profit. If you are to stay in business as a contractor, you must make sufficient profit above the break-even point to allow you to acquire enough operating capital to secure your business and work toward future expansion.

Essay Questions

CHAPTER 5

Notes

1. What have you determined once your bid price covers all of your job costs and what does that mean?

2. The estimated labor hours must be adjusted for working conditions. Think of as many job conditions that effect labor units that you can and list them here.

3. How do you determine the estimated labor cost for a job?

4. What two methods are used to determine the labor rate per man-hour?

5. Where is labor burden applied to the estimate?

6. What is the second step in determining your break-even cost?

Notes

7. Direct job expenses are those often not shown on the drawings but they need to be included in the estimate. List as many of these expenses as you can think of.

8. What is "Estimated Prime Cost" and for what is it used?

9. What is the cost related to the operation and management of the company known as?

10. What are the two methods of applying overhead to a job?

11. How do you determine your break-even cost?

CHAPTER 5

Multiple-Choice Questions

Notes

5.1 Labor Hours

1. Determining labor adjustments comes with experience and is part of what makes estimating _____.

   (a) a science
   (b) difficult
   (c) an art form
   (d) easy

2. After you have adjusted the total labor-unit hours, you must consider any additional _____ for the job that might apply.

   (a) labor requirements
   (b) miscellaneous material
   (c) material requirements
   (d) none of these

5.2 Labor Cost

3. The actual labor cost for a job is determined by multiplying the total adjusted labor man-hours by the labor rate per man-hour.

   (a) True
   (b) False

5.3 Labor Rate per Man-Hour

4. The shop average labor rate per man-hour is determined by _____ the total field labor cost over a given period of time by the total number of field man-hours over the same period of time.

   (a) adding
   (b) subtracting
   (c) multiplying
   (d) dividing

Notes

5. Another approach in determining the labor rate per man-hour is to use the anticipated _____ labor rate per man-hour.

(a) prevailing
(b) job average
(c) union scale
(d) cheapest possible

5.4 Labor Burden

6. In addition to the cost of labor, other costs associated with labor that must be taken into consideration are identified as "_____" costs.

(a) employee benefit
(b) Workers' Comp
(c) labor burden
(d) all of these

5.5 Total Material Cost

7. The second step in determining your break-even cost is to transfer the _____ from the Price/Labor Worksheets to the Estimate Summary Worksheet.

(a) lighting fixtures and switch gear
(b) miscellaneous material
(c) sales tax and small tools
(d) material cost

8. Add a percentage to the total cost of material as an adjustment for miscellaneous material. An addition of _____ percent of the material cost as a factor is suggested when you are doing the estimate manually.

(a) 10
(b) 11
(c) 12
(d) 13

Notes

9. A factor of ______ percent of the total material cost is considered an acceptable value for small tools.

(a) 1
(b) 2
(c) 3
(d) 4

5.6 Direct Job Expenses

10. Step three in determining the break-even cost is to account for ______ expenses which are often not shown on the drawings, but probably indicated in the specifications.

(a) lighting fixtures and switch gear
(b) direct job
(c) sales tax and small tools
(d) profit

5.7 Estimated Prime Cost

11. "______" is simply a term used to identify the subtotaled cost of labor, material, and direct costs.

(a) Estimated Prime Cost
(b) Overhead Cost
(c) Profit
(d) Job Cost

5.8 Overhead

12. The cost related to the operation and management of the company such as rent, insurance, vehicles, administrative salaries, professional fees, and so on, is known as "______."

(a) overhead
(b) profit
(c) labor burden
(d) none of these

Notes

5.9 Overhead Calculation Methods

13. Most contractors apply overhead as a ____.

(a) percentage of prime cost
(b) rate per labor-hour
(c) factor of labor burden
(d) percentage of profit

14. Since overhead is related primarily to the management of labor and not the cost of material, overhead should be applied to the ____.

(a) prime cost
(b) labor man-hours of a job
(c) labor burden
(d) profit

5.10 Break-Even Cost (Estimated Cost)

15. To determine the break-even cost, all you need to do is add the cost of labor, material, direct job expenses, overhead, and profit together.

(a) True
(b) False

CHAPTER 6 THE BID PROCESS

INTRODUCTION

High bids can cause you to lose the sales that your company depends on. Low bids can win sales, but cause the loss of profits or the demise of the company. Between these two losing propositions is the "accurate" bid—and that is the only kind of bid you want to produce.

An accurate bid is important;

- Helps lock in profits.
- Eliminates built-in loss of revenue or profit.
- Provides a means for knocking low bids out of the competition.
- Reduces cash-flow problems.
- Reduces resource conflicts.
- Provides the highest return on the bidding effort.
- Provides accurate information for negotiation to win a job or support changes.
- Reduces risk.

It is important that you understand what a "winning bid" actually is. Many people think it is the one that lands the job, but quite often, the winning bid is actually the "losing" bid, because the company that won the job by under-bidding did not win anything but financial loss.

A winning bid is one of two things:

- It lands you a profitable job that your company can handle.
- It prevents you from taking on a losing project.

A losing bid is one of two things:

- It prevents you from taking on a profitable project that your company can handle because the bid was too high.
- It lands you a losing project because the bid was too low.

Your company might not be able to handle a job due to resource constraints, lack of expertise, conflicts with other projects, or any number of other factors. Most of these factors will not be identified in any document your company has. Nor will any alarm bells ring to notify you that something is out of kilter. You have to discover and

Notes

quantify these things by analysis. In this chapter, we will provide a methodology for performing that analysis.

Now, armed with your knowledge of the estimating process and how to determine the break-even point, you just need to know how to properly prepare a winning bid. That is what you will learn next.

6.1 Profit (It Is Not a Dirty Word)

Net profit is the bottom line. It is a report card against which all business persons are measured. A winning bid includes a reasonable amount for profit.

How Much Profit Is Reasonable?

A reasonable profit margin will be whatever the market will bear without gouging the customer. Some factors to consider include:

- Competition and the Economy
- Management/Organization
- Job Size
- Risk
- Speed of Payment

Competition and the Economy. Consider the number of competitors who are expected to be bidding on the job and their experience in the particular line of work. When the construction market is in a recession or the market is shrinking, a highly competitive market develops and competition for jobs drives the selling price down. If the economy is strong or the market is expanding, prices and profits typically increase. This all happens according to the law of supply-and-demand. Consider increasing your profit margins when you are busy, and lowering them when you are slow; sometimes it is just that simple.

Management/Organization. Profitable contracting demands that the job be sold for more than what it will cost to complete. To meet this goal, you must manage your resources in an efficient and effective manner and keep your costs down. If you do, your prices should be competitive, even with a profit margin exceeding that of your competitors.

Job Size. The generally accepted practice is that smaller jobs are sold with higher profit margins, as compared to larger jobs.

Notes

Risk. When doing an unfamiliar job, you might need to increase your profit margin to cover the risk of completing the project within the price of the estimate. However, the risk factor might not be the same for your competitors, thus allowing them to submit a lower bid.

Speed of Payment. Consider how quickly you are likely to be paid. If there is likely to be an extended amount of time involved, then you might need to consider the cost of financing your investment in the job.

6.2 Profit to Prime Cost

Most contractors apply profit as a percentage of break-even cost, so be sure to use a markup multiplier, not the percent of profit to sales value from the financial statement!

Small Size Contractor Income Statement Year Ending December 31		
Sales	$250,000	100% of Sales
Direct Job Cost		
Labor (4,000 Hrs)	$80,000	
Material	$70,000	
Total Direct Cost	$150,000	60% of Sales
Gross Profit	$100,000	40% of Sales
Overhead Expenses (Administrative Cost)		
Salaries and Commissions	$15,000	
Advertising	$5,000	
Auto and Gas	$10,000	
Benefits	$20,000	
Interest	$1,000	
Insurance—Auto, General, Workers' Comp.	$5,000	
Miscellaneous Expense	$3,000	
Payroll Taxes	$8,000	
Rent	$5,000	
Utilities/Phone	$3,000	
Total Administrative Expenses (50% of Prime)	$75,000	30% of Sales
Net Profit Before Taxes (16.67% of Prime)	**$25,000**	**10% of Sales**

Notes

Profit Multiplier									
% of Sales	Multiplier	% of Sales	Multiplier	% of Sales	Multiplier	% of Sales	Multiplier	% of Sales	Multiplier
5%	5.26%	10%	11.11%	15%	17.65%	20%	25.00%	25%	33.33%
6%	6.38%	11%	12.36%	16%	19.05%	21%	26.58%	26%	35.14%
7%	7.53%	12%	13.64%	17%	20.48%	22%	28.21%	27%	36.99%
8%	8.70%	13%	14.94%	18%	21.95%	23%	29.87%	28%	38.89%
9%	9.89%	14%	16.28%	19%	23.46%	24%	31.58%	29%	40.85%
Multiplier Formula = ((1/(1 - % of sales)) - 1) x 100									

Profit		
Description	Value	To Sales
Labor Cost	$1,975.86	26.23%
Labor Burden (Included When Overhead is Applied)	$0.00	0.00%
Material Cost	$2,278.20	30.24%
Direct Job Cost	$550.00	7.30%
Estimated Prime Cost	$4,804.06	63.77%
Overhead, (Hrs x Rate per Hour)	$1,975.86	26.23%
Break Even	$6,779.92	90.00%
Profit 10% of Sales (Markup 11.11%)	**$753.25**	**10.00%**
Bid Price	**$7,533.17**	**100.00%**

6.3 Other Bid Cost Considerations

Be sure you review the plans and specifications one final time before submitting your bid, and make sure you understand all of the bid conditions, such as:

Completion Penalty. Some projects may have penalties such as $500 to $1,000 for each day past the scheduled completion date, essentially a punishment for not being done on time. You need to consider these costs when you determine your final bid price. Look at the anticipated job schedule and your list of specialty items, such as switchgear, panels, a generator, lighting fixtures, or other items that will likely need to be special ordered. Find out from the vendors what the anticipated lead time is, and allow some time for the submittal and approval process, perhaps a month. Now look at where the delivery dates fall within the job schedule. Will there be sufficient time to install the items before the scheduled completion date? It may be worthwhile to put a qualification in your proposal about an availability issue related to the job schedule.

Most states and the federal government have outlawed completion penalties; however, the owners are permitted to seek compensation for their out-of-pocket expenses. These expenses are referred to as "Liquidated Damages."

Finance Cost. Be sure to include the cost to finance the job if this is applicable. For example, the cost of borrowing $25,000 at an interest rate of 10 percent for a year is $2,500.

Liquidated Damages. The most common component of a Liquidated Damage clause is the calculated cost to the owner arising from each day of delay. That amount is then set forth in the bidding and contract documents. Some documents may limit the owner to recovering a specific amount; however, some allow for complete recovery if the calculated amount falls short. Also, in cases where there has been blatant disregard by a contractor to perform, the owner may file suit for additional damages. It is important to pay close attention to the verbiage of Liquidated Damage clauses.

In the courts, Liquidated Damages cases have not been dealt with in a consistent manner. In the United States, the courts have tended not to enforce the Liquidated Damages clause if the stipulated amount exceeds the actual loss, but have required compensation for the actual harm suffered.

Retainage Cost. Some jobs require that a portion of each payment (typically 10 percent) be held for a specific period of time (typically 90 to 180 days) after the final electrical inspection; and some require a portion be held for the duration of your warranty period.

The purpose of the owner holding back the money (Retainage) is to guarantee that the electrical system has been installed correctly and according to the contract before all final payments have been released. You might want to add the cost of money you do not have access to.

Example: *Retainage cost (10%) for 180 days for a $250,000 project will be $1,500 at an interest rate of 12 percent.*

Cost = ($250,000 x 10%) x (12% x 0.50)
Cost = ($25,000) x (6%)
Cost = $1,500 or 0.01% of the selling price

Author's Comment: This value might be insignificant to some, but somebody is going to pay for this. Then again, it might already have been included when you applied overhead.

Notes

Notes

Submitted Bid Price	
Labor Cost (Hrs x Rate) (109.77 x $18.00)	$1,975.86
Labor Burden (Included When Overhead is Applied)	$0.00
Material Cost	$2,278.20
Direct Job Cost	$550.00
Estimated Prime Cost	$4,804.06
Overhead, (Hrs x Rate per Hour)	$1,975.86
Break Even	$6,779.92
Profit 10% of Sales (Markup multiplier 11.11%)	$753.25
Bid Price	**$7,533.17**
Other Bid Considerations	
Completion Penalty Allowance	$0.00
Finance Cost (part of overhead)	$0.00
Liquidated Damages Allowance	$0.00
Retainage Cost Allowance	$0.00
Other	$0.00
Submitted Bid Price	**$7,533.17**

6.4 Bid Accuracy

To ensure that your bid is accurate, you need to verify that you have not made any of the following errors:

- Assuming standard-grade devices, when specification grade is required
- Errors in math or calculations
- Failure to review jobsite conditions, especially for retrofit jobs
- Failure to comply with specifications or drawing notes
- Forgetting a major item, such as a switchgear or subcontractor quote
- Forgetting to include outside or underground work
- Not transferring totals properly from page to page
- Omitting a section of the estimate, like an entire floor
- Using improper estimating forms that lead to errors
- Using supplier take-off quantities for quotes
- Relying on verbal supplier quotes
- Not verifying that quotes (for example fixtures or switchgear) match the schedules or specifications

- Using the wrong scale on reduced size drawings
- Using the wrong labor unit
- Using the wrong material cost

Notes

6.5 Bid Analysis

Before you submit your bid to the customer, do as much bid analysis as you can to ensure that your bid is as accurate as possible and that nothing fell through the cracks.

Average Branch Raceway Length per Outlet

A quick check worth doing is to divide the total footage of branch raceways by the number of outlets. This type of an analysis can be applied to each phase of a project such as fire alarm systems, sound systems, and so forth.

Average Branch Circuit Length per Outlet			
Outlets		**Branch Raceways**	
Fluorescent Fixtures	18	1/2 EMT 2 - 12 AWG	662
Recessed Lights	24	1/2 EMT 3 - 12 AWG	91
Exit Lights	2	1/2 EMT 4 - 12 AWG	128
Switch Outlets	4	1/2 EMT 5 - 12 AWG	10
Receptacle Outlet	9	Total 1/2 EMT	891
IG Receptacle Outlet	2		
Total	**59**	**Run per Outlet**	**15.10**

Average Number of Wires per Raceway Foot

Another quick check is to divide branch-circuit wiring by branch raceway lengths. If the answer is less than 2 or more than 4, that is a warning sign to check for errors.

Notes

Avg. # of Wires per Raceway Ft	
Branch Raceways	
1/2 EMT 2 - 12 AWG	662
1/2 EMT 3 - 12 AWG	91
1/2 EMT 4 - 12 AWG	128
1/2 EMT 5 - 12 AWG	10
Total 1/2 EMT	**891**
Run per Outlet	**15.10**
12 AWG	2,393
Average per EMT Ft	**2.69**

Percent Distribution to Selling Price

Check the percentage distribution of labor, material, direct cost, overhead, and profit to sales. Be sure you do this for all jobs so that you can compare each bid against previously completed jobs of a similar nature.

Percent Distribution to Selling Price		
Description	**Value**	**To Sales**
Labor Cost	$1,975.86	26.23%
Labor Burden (Included When Overhead is Applied)	$0.00	0.00%
Material Cost	$2,278.20	30.24%
Direct Job Cost	$550.00	7.30%
Estimated Prime Cost	$4,804.06	63.77%
Overhead, (Hrs x Rate per Hour)	$1,975.86	26.23%
Break Even	$6,779.92	90.00%
Profit 10% of Sales (Markup 11.11%)	$753.25	10.00%
Bid Price	**$7,533.17**	**100.00%**

Cost per Square Foot

Another check is to calculate the cost per square foot; simply divide the selling price by the square footage of the building.

Notes

Example: The cost per square foot for the 2,500 sq ft meeting room is $3.01 [$7,533.17/2,500 sq ft], or a ballpark price of $3.00 per square foot.

Author's Comment: The cost per square foot values can be used to check an estimate for validity, not as the basis for a bid.

Cost per Labor Hour

Another check is to calculate the cost per labor hour; simply divide the selling price by the number of labor hours.

Example: The cost per labor hour for the 2,500 sq ft meeting room is $68.63 [$7,533.17/109.77 hours], or a ballpark price of $70 per labor hour.

Author's Comment: The cost per labor hour values can be used to check an estimate for validity, not as the basis for a bid.

Labor Days

One final consideration is how the job will be staffed (number of man-days) and if this information appears to be valid. You determine this by dividing the total job hours by the number of hours per day that the job will be staffed.

Example: The meeting room is estimated to take 109.77 hours, if we plan on working 16 hours per day (two electricians), the job should take 6.86 labor days [109.77 hours/16 hours].

Experience

As an estimator develops his or her skills and accumulates history, he or she will be able to develop more of these quick checks and reduce the risk of errors.

6.6 Bid Proposal

When the bid is complete, you must submit a written proposal that clarifies what the bid includes and what it does not. The following is a sample of what your proposal might look like:

Notes

Proposal/Quotation for Electrical Work

April 1, 20xx

Owner/Contractor
Mike Holt Enterprises, Inc.
352-360-2620 (c), 352-360-0983 (f)
3604 Parkway Blvd. Suite 3
Leesburg, Florida 34748

Project Location
3604 Parkway Blvd., Suite 3
Leesburg, Florida 34748

Scope of Work: Wire meeting room as per drawing and supply all electrical fixtures and wiring devices as per the following:

Fixtures	
Fluorescent Lay-In	18
Recessed	24
Exit	2
Switches	
Switch—Single Pole (1-Gang)	1
Switch—3-Way (1-Gang)	1
Switch—Two Single-Pole (2-Gang)	1
Switch—One Single-Pole & One 3-Way (2-Gang)	1
Receptacles	
Receptacle 20A, 125V	9
Receptacle IG 20A, 125V	2
Total Outlets	59
Cost	**$7,533.17**

Terms and Conditions

Plans/Specifications – Electrical work requested by others not indicated on plans and/or specifications shall not be part of this agreement.

Change Orders – Deviation or alteration to the scope of this agreement, including plans or specifications, shall be executed on receipt of written orders.

Design Errors – Wiring modifications required because of errors in design by the architect and/or engineer shall be considered a change order.

Notes

Proposal/Quotation for Electrical Work (continued)

April 1, 20xx

Equipment Supplied by Others – Electrical Contractor shall not be responsible for the installation, damage, theft, vandalism, storage, or warranty of equipment supplied by others.

Codes and Installation Practices – Material and equipment supplied by Electrical Contractor shall be installed in accordance with the *National Electrical Code*, local electrical building code, and standard electrical practices. Requirements that are not codified as of the date of this proposal are excluded from this quotation.

Payment and Terms – Payment(s) not received according to an approved payment schedule shall be considered past due, and Electrical Contractor will not perform any work until all past-due payments are current.

Performance – Electrical Contractor will not work after 5 p.m. or weekends (overtime) unless authorized in writing by owner/contractor via a signed change order.

Permit – The cost of the permit shall be paid by owner.

Repairs – Electrical Contractor shall not be responsible for any work associated with the repair of concrete/drywall, including painting, patching, and sealing of roof penetrations as required for the installation of electrical wiring and equipment.

Temporary Power – None to be supplied by Electrical Contractor.

Termination of Agreement – This agreement shall remain in effect for 365 days from the date of signing of this agreement by the owner/contractor and Electrical Contractor.

Warranty – Warranty of electrical material and equipment supplied by Electrical Contractor shall be for a period of one year from date of final invoice. No warranty will be provided for material and equipment supplied by others, and no warranty shall be performed while invoice(s), including change order(s) are past due.

Waste – Electrical Contractor supplied waste shall be removed to a specific area on the construction site as instructed by the owner/contractor.

This proposal/quotation does not become legal and binding unless signed by both parties.

____ Date: _____/_____/_____

Owner/Contractor

____ Date: _____/_____/_____

Mike Holt Enterprises, Inc

CHAPTER 6

Summary

Notes

Introduction

High bids can cause you to lose the sales that your company depends on. Low bids can win sales, but cause the loss of profits or the demise of the company. Between these two losing propositions is the "accurate" bid—and that is the only kind of bid you want to produce.

The accurate bid:

- Helps lock in profits.
- Eliminates built-in loss of revenue or profit.
- Provides a means for knocking low bids out of the competition.
- Reduces cash-flow problems.
- Reduces resource conflicts.
- Provides the highest return on the bidding effort.
- Provides accurate information for negotiation to win a job or support changes
- Reduces risk.

It is important that you understand what a "winning bid" actually is. It is one of two things:

- It lands you a profitable job that your company can handle.
- It prevents you from taking on a losing project.

A losing bid is one of two things:

- It prevents you from taking on a profitable project that your company can handle because the bid was too high.
- It lands you a losing project because the bid was too low.

6.1 Profit (It Is Not a Dirty Word)

A reasonable profit margin will be whatever the market will bear without gouging the customer. Some factors to consider include:

- Competition and the Economy
- Management/Organization
- Job Size
- Risk
- Speed of Payment

6.2 Profit to Prime Cost

Notes

Most contractors apply profit as a percentage of break-even cost, so be sure to use a markup multiplier, not the percent of profit to sales value from the financial statement!

6.3 Other Bid Cost Considerations

Be sure you review the plans and specifications one final time before submitting your bid, and make sure you understand all of the bid conditions, such as:

- Completion Penalty
- Finance Cost
- Liquidated Damages
- Retainage Cost

6.4 Bid Accuracy

To ensure that your bid is accurate, you need to verify that you have not made any of the following errors:

- Assuming standard-grade devices, when specification grade is required
- Errors in math or calculations
- Failure to review jobsite conditions, especially for retrofit jobs
- Failure to comply with specifications or drawing notes
- Forgetting a major item, such as a switchgear or subcontractor quote
- Forgetting to include outside or underground work
- Not transferring totals properly from page to page
- Omitting a section of the estimate, like an entire floor!
- Using improper estimating forms that lead to errors
- Using supplier take-off quantities for quotes
- Relying on verbal supplier quotes
- Not verifying that quotes (for example fixtures or switchgear) match the schedules or specifications
- Using the wrong scale on reduced size drawings
- Using the wrong labor unit
- Using the wrong material cost

Notes

6.5 Bid Analysis

Before you submit your bid to the customer, do as much bid analysis as you can to ensure that your bid is as accurate as possible and that nothing fell through the cracks. Types of analyses include:

- Average Branch Raceway Length per Outlet
- Average Number of Wires per Raceway Foot
- Percent Distribution to Selling Price
- Cost per Square Foot
- Cost per Labor Hour
- Labor Days

6.6 Bid Proposal

When the bid is complete, you must submit a written proposal that clarifies what the bid includes and what it does not.

CHAPTER 6

Conclusion

Notes

You have come a long way in a short time. You have now learned how to produce an estimate, determine the break-even point, and develop a bid. You have learned how to do those things accurately, efficiently, and thoroughly.

Because you have traded guesswork for methodology, you have traded risk for opportunity and you have traded uncertainty for confidence. For this reason, your reputation should grow right along with your company's profits.

Next, we are going to show you a time-saving method called "unit pricing."

CHAPTER 6

Essay Questions

Notes

1. What benefits does an accurate bid provide to a company?

2. What is a winning bid?

3. What is a losing bid?

4. What are some factors that should be considered when determining a reasonable profit margin?

5. When applying profit as a percentage of break-even cost, what should be used?

6. What are some of the bid conditions you need to be sure you understand before submitting your bid?

7. What errors should you check for to ensure your bid is accurate?

8. What are some types of bid analyses you should do before submitting your bid to the customer?

9. What must you do when the bid is complete?

Notes

CHAPTER 6

Multiple-Choice Questions

Notes

Introduction

1. The "_____" bid is the only kind of bid you want to produce.

   (a) highest
   (b) lowest
   (c) accurate
   (d) best

6.1 Profit (It Is Not a Dirty Word)

2. A reasonable profit margin will be whatever _____ without gouging the customer.

   (a) the market will bear
   (b) the customer will accept
   (c) management dictates
   (d) any of these

3. If the economy is strong or the market is expanding, prices and profits typically _____.

   (a) remain stable
   (b) decrease
   (c) increase
   (d) fluctuate

6.2 Profit to Prime Cost

4. Most contractors apply profit as a percentage of break-even cost, so be sure to use a markup multiplier, not the percent of profit to sales value from the _____!

   (a) balance sheet
   (b) financial statement
   (c) sales analysis report
   (d) return on investment analysis

6.3 Other Bid Cost Considerations

Notes

5. Be sure you review the plans and specifications one final time before ______, and make sure you understand all of the bid conditions.

   (a) submitting your bid
   (b) planning your proposal
   (c) applying profit and overhead
   (d) considering labor burden

6.4 Bid Accuracy

6. To ensure that your bid is accurate, you need to verify that you have not made any of the typical errors.

   (a) True
   (b) False

6.5 Bid Analysis

7. Before you ______, do as much bid analysis as you can to ensure that your bid is as accurate as possible and that nothing fell through the cracks.

   (a) prepare the final proposal
   (b) determine your break-even cost
   (c) apply profit
   (d) submit your bid to the customer

8. A quick check worth doing is to ______ the total footage of branch raceways ______ the number of outlets.

   (a) add, to
   (b) subtract, from
   (c) multiply, by
   (d) divide, by

Notes

9. Another quick check is to divide branch-circuit wiring by branch raceway lengths. If the answer is less than 2 or more than _____, that is a warning sign to check for errors.

(a) 3
(b) 4
(c) 5
(d) 6

10. You should also check the percentage distribution of labor, material, direct cost, overhead, and profit to sales.

(a) True
(b) False

6.6 Bid Proposal

11. When the bid is complete, you must submit a _____ proposal that clarifies what the bid includes and what it does not.

(a) verbal
(b) written
(c) a or b
(d) a and b

UNIT PRICING

INTRODUCTION

Now that you have learned the detailed estimating method and bid process, we are going to show you an alternative estimating method. It is called "unit pricing," and using it will save you time. You can safely use unit pricing on renovations, office build-outs, change orders, and other simple or small-scope jobs.

7.1 What Is Unit Pricing?

Unit pricing consists of developing an average price to install a given electrical component, such as a duplex receptacle, a 2 x 4 fluorescent fixture, or a switch. This price includes the outlet box, an average number of wire connectors, mounting hardware, and the typical number of raceway or cable box connectors. The "unit price" is then multiplied by the number of units on the drawings to arrive at a total bid price for the installation.

7.2 Advantages and Disadvantages of Unit Pricing

You still do a take-off to determine the number of luminaries, switches, receptacles, and so forth. However, you just do not separately count the boxes, fittings, and other parts included in the unit pricing components. Often you do not measure the wiring runs for every opening, but use an average length per installed outlet as part of the "unit."

Homeruns to panelboards, communications cabinets, and so on, must still be measured in the usual manner.

Advantages

Unit pricing is faster and easier than the detailed estimating method described earlier in Chapters 4, 5, and 6. It takes less time and therefore costs your company less money to determine the selling price for a job.

Unit pricing is relatively accurate on repetitive jobs where many identical items of electrical equipment will be installed under the same (or fairly similar) conditions.

Notes

Disadvantages

Unit pricing is not suitable for jobs where outlets are not located at standard intervals. For example, if you have 200 identical fluorescent luminaries to install in a building where the ceiling heights vary from 8 ft to 15 ft in different areas, unit prices will need to be adjusted to an average luminaire height, or different unit prices will need to be applied for the different ceiling heights.

7.3 Unit Price Example

It is easier to demonstrate this concept with an example rather than trying to explain it in words.

Determine the unit price for a duplex receptacle based on the following factors:

- Labor Hour Adjustment—10%
- Labor Burden—included in overhead
- Labor Rate—$18 per man-hour
- Material Cost Adjustment—15% (waste, theft, miscellaneous)
- Sales Tax—7%
- Overhead—$18 per man-hour
- Profit—15% of Selling Price

Notes

Unit Cost—Single-Pole Switch								
				Extension	Labor	Extension		
Item #	Item Description	Qty	Cost	Cost	Unit	Hrs	Unit	
31	Metal Boxes 4 x 4" Regular	1	$47.84	$0.48	18.00	0.18	100	
1711	Rings, 1-Gang	1	$39.00	$0.39	4.50	0.05	100	
315	EMT Set Screw Connectors ½"	2	$9.43	$0.19	2.00	0.04	100	
305	EMT ½"	20	$19.39	$3.88	2.25	0.45	100	
355	EMT Set Screw Couplings ½"	1	$9.70	$0.10	2.00	0.02	100	
415	EMT Straps 1-Hole ½"	3	$3.10	$0.09	2.50	0.08	100	
2091	Switches—15A, 125V, 1-Pole	1	$58.23	$0.58	20.00	0.20	100	
1261	Plates, Plastic 1-Gang Switch	1	$18.88	$0.19	2.50	0.03	100	
2391	Wire—12 THHN, Copper, 600V	50	$73.69	$3.68	4.25	0.21	1,000	
				$9.58		1.26 hr		
Labor								
	Labor Hours with Adjustment	10%				1.39 hr		
	Labor Cost	$18.00					$25.02	34.40%
Material								
	Material Cost with Adjustment	15%		$11.02				
	Sales Tax	7%		$0.77				
	Material Cost						$11.79	16.21%
Unit Price Summary								
	Prime Cost (Material + Labor)						$36.81	50.60%
	Overhead	$18.00					$25.02	34.40%
	Break-Even Cost						$61.83	85.00%
	Profit 15% (17.65% Markup Multiplier)	17.65%					$10.91	14.83%
	Unit Price						$72.74	100.00%

CHAPTER 7

Summary

Notes

Introduction

An alternative estimating method is called "unit pricing," and using it will save you time. You can safely use unit pricing on renovations, office build-outs, change orders, and other simple or small-scope jobs.

7.1 What is Unit Pricing?

Unit pricing consists of developing an average price to install a given electrical component. This price includes the outlet box, an average number of wire connectors, mounting hardware, and the typical number of raceway or cable box connectors. The "unit price" is then multiplied by the number of units on the drawings to arrive at a total bid price for the installation.

7.2 Advantages and Disadvantages of Unit Pricing

You still do a take-off to determine the number of luminaries, switches, receptacles, and so forth. However, you just do not separately count the boxes, fittings, and other parts included in the unit pricing components. Often you do not measure the wiring runs for every opening, but use an average length per installed outlet as part of the "unit."

Homeruns to panelboards, communications cabinets, and so on, must still be measured in the usual manner.

Advantages. Unit pricing is faster and easier than the detailed estimating method. It takes less time and therefore costs your company less money to determine the selling price for a job.

Unit pricing is relatively accurate on repetitive jobs where many identical items of electrical equipment will be installed under the same (or fairly similar) conditions.

Disadvantages. Unit pricing is not suitable for jobs where outlets are not located at standard intervals.

CHAPTER

7

Conclusion

Notes

From the example, you can see that the unit pricing method can be a real time saver. Do not let this lull you into trading time for the accuracy required for estimating projects that are not small or simple. Even minor variations in the work environment can call for adjustments to the unit pricing method.

Your company can use other costing and pricing methods as well. All of these have limited applications. Going outside the limits of these methods, or of unit pricing, can result in large financial losses.

As you practice the unit pricing method and the more rigorous detailed estimating method you learned earlier, you will become more adept at each. The first few times you use the unit pricing method, you may also want to use the more rigorous detailed method and compare the results.

CHAPTER 7

Essay Questions

Notes

1. What is an alternative estimating method called that will save you time, and on what types of jobs can it be safely used?

2. What does the average unit price include?

3. When using unit pricing, what must still be measured in the usual manner?

4. What are the advantages of using unit pricing?

5. What are the disadvantages of using unit pricing?

CHAPTER 7

Multiple-Choice Questions

Notes

Introduction

1. An alternative to the detailed estimating method and bid process is called the "______" method.

   (a) square foot
   (b) unit pricing
   (c) shot-in-the-dark
   (d) none of these

7.1 What Is Unit Pricing?

2. Unit pricing consists of developing a(n) ______ price to install a given electrical component.

   (a) set
   (b) estimated
   (c) average
   (d) flexible

3. The "unit price" is ______ by the number of units on the drawings to arrive at a total bid price for the installation.

   (a) added
   (b) subtracted
   (c) multiplied
   (d) divided

7.2 Advantages and Disadvantages of Unit Pricing

4. The biggest advantage when using unit pricing is that you do not need to complete a take-off to determine the number of luminaries, switches, receptacles, and so forth.

   (a) True
   (b) False

Notes

5. Unit pricing is relatively accurate on repetitive jobs where many _____ items of electrical equipment will be installed under the same (or fairly similar) conditions.

   (a) identical
   (b) individual
   (c) unique
   (d) all of these

6. Unit pricing is not suitable for jobs where outlets are not located at standard intervals.

   (a) True
   (b) False

CHAPTER 8

SOFTWARE-BASED ESTIMATING

INTRODUCTION

The previous chapters have taught you how to produce a manual estimate and bid accurately and effectively. This chapter will help you better make use of estimating software. It is important to remember that software is a tool, and cannot by itself ensure your success. Estimating software allows estimators to improve accuracy, consistency, and speed when preparing estimates. These benefits lead to improved project management and increased profitability. But it does have its limits. It cannot replace your judgment or experience, nor can it replace your knowledge of electrical installations or of the particular installation for which you are preparing an estimate.

8.1 Computer Estimating System Functions

Take-Off

A standard computer-assisted estimating system requires the estimator to take the time to learn how it works and, in addition, requires effort to build the right items or assemblies in the database. The additional information required by computer-assisted estimating systems considers the type of construction, whereas the manual counting method uses an accepted figure regardless of the construction type. However, once an assembly is built, it can be used repeatedly (as long as prices are updated), and this will help to speed up the estimating process.

Most systems will have a database of parts and assemblies included in the software product, but someone must take time to verify the assemblies, material prices, and labor units. Once verified, a well setup database can increase the speed and accuracy of the take-off.

Someone must assign the proper breakout or section of the bid prior to entering data. A "count entry" function requires typing in and/or clicking a button for the correct value. This can be more work than handwriting a symbol or note and then placing a figure underneath it.

Some estimators still use the manual take-off to a paper system and then enter the information into the computer. Computer system and software developers are creating new tools for performing the take-off. One type uses a scanning process but it is currently still too sensitive and unreliable. Another allows for screen take-off with the mouse and it is reliable but requires a larger monitor and in some cases two of them.

Notes

An accurate automatic take-off system is available for taking off quantities from AUTOCAD drawings but owners and engineers are resisting making the electronic drawings available for bidding purposes.

Extensions

Manual. The manual method requires a detailed write-up and expansion of the counted items. A duplex receptacle has at least nine individual components that need to be written down, along with their associated material prices and labor units. Then these values need to be calculated against the quantities, and subtotals need to be entered for each. After all this, final totals need to be summed up.

This takes a great deal of time, effort, accuracy, and hand strength. After all this, someone else will need to double-check the extensions for accuracy. Imagine the time required to complete this process on a bid that has three or more bid forms. Worse, imagine what has to be done if something changes or a mistake is found after these final extensions are created.

Manual Extensions

Item Description	Qty	Cost	Extension Cost	Labor Hours	Extension Hours	Unit
Metal Boxes 4 x 4" Regular	1	$47.84	$0.48	18.00	0.18	100
Rings, 1-Gang	1	$39.00	$0.39	4.50	0.05	100
EMT Set Screw Connectors ½"	2	$9.43	$0.19	2.00	0.04	100
EMT ½"	20	$19.39	$3.88	2.25	0.45	100
EMT Set Screw Couplings ½"	1	$9.70	$0.10	2.00	0.02	100
EMT Straps 1-Hole ½"	3	$3.10	$0.09	2.50	0.08	100
Switches—15A, 125V, 1-Pole	1	$58.23	$0.58	20.00	0.20	100
Plates, Plastic 1-Gang Switch	1	$18.88	$0.19	2.50	0.03	100
Wire—12 THHN, Copper, 600V	50	$73.69	$3.68	4.25	0.21	1,000
Totals			**9.58**		**1.26**	

With Software. With estimating software, the extension phase becomes a simple mouse click or two. The computer does the rest with more accuracy and speed than any human (or even a large group of humans) ever could. If something changes or a mistake is found, it is much easier to make the necessary corrections and redo the extensions.

Notes

8.2 Advantages and Benefits

Estimating software does not eliminate the need to learn how to estimate. Using software can make a good estimator far more effective. An unskilled estimator is still going to do a poor job of estimating, regardless of whether estimating software is used or not.

Better Use of Your Time

A computer does thousands of mathematical computations in a fraction of a second, never makes a mathematical error, never becomes tired or careless, and never forgets the information that is stored in it. Estimating software reduces estimating time and costs, partly because you no longer need to price, labor, extend, or total material and labor manually.

This translates into additional time for other important functions such as more time to review an estimate, to bid more jobs, to better organize and manage the company, or to spend more time with family.

Better Control of Material Cost

Once the take-off is complete and you have entered the quantities, you can easily generate a report of all the material required for the job. You can generate a summary or a report broken down by job phase or type of materials. You can then e-mail this to multiple suppliers so you can obtain competitive prices and fixed delivery dates. You can also share the estimate with a contractor's purchasing and accounting departments. Cost tracking and inventory control become much simpler when you use software to generate and control the information. Material prices can be changed easily, quickly, and accurately at the last minute.

You can make information secure and easier to retrieve with various search criteria specific to what you are looking for. You vastly reduce the investment in office space and filing cabinets, while reducing the fire fuel load that comes with storing large quantities of paper. But what if you do have a fire? A software-based system with remote backup means your information is safely out of harm's way.

A computer-based estimating system also provides for easy accumulation of project history that can be used to evaluate the accuracy of each new estimate.

Notes

Better Project Management

If integrated properly with the project management system, estimating software provides the flexibility to track projects in many ways, such as by system, floor, building, site, or project phase. A project manager can make a few mouse clicks to update the Work Breakdown Structure, Critical Path, Gant Chart, and other key project management items in real time.

It is easy to share information with people in the field. Keeping the field supervisors apprised of the current labor budget, material information, and daily schedule updates help them complete work on time. The project manager can decide which reports to send out so that people in the field are not overwhelmed by information they do not need.

Estimating software can also help supervisors in the field order material and better control its arrival at the jobsite. This reduces handling time, improves inventory control, reduces storage and theft problems, and assists with other issues that stem from inefficient material handling practices.

It is important to be sure an estimate is accurate and error free before using it for project management. Some companies require a re-estimate of a project after it is awarded.

Reduced Overhead

The ability of an estimator to bid more jobs in the same amount of time reduces estimating costs relative to revenue. Material inventory control improves, providing such benefits as reduced costs for storage space and financing. You can also improve billing and expedite collections. All of this will increase cash flow, which may further reduce your costs of capital and/or allow you to use your capital more effectively.

Increased Profitability for Your Business

The savings in estimating time will permit you to estimate more jobs. That, in turn, will allow you to expand business volume. Increasing volume, in itself, is not always good. Increasing the volume of profitable jobs is the real goal, and good software can help you do that.

Computer-assisted estimates can improve your marketing program and sales efforts because they can provide you with a more detailed and professional looking package to present to customers. This, however, is only the beginning of what you can do.

You can provide a level of detail that shows what is actually required to complete the job, along with price breakdowns that show lowball bids cannot be taken seriously. Yes, you will still be competing with any bidders that also prepare an accurate estimate. But that is really what the bidding process is supposed to achieve in the first place.

Notes

When you submit a sufficiently detailed bid, you give your customers more reason to be confident in your company's knowledge of their projects and ability to complete those projects in a timely and competent manner. This confidence in your company's preparation will result in more requests for bids, and ultimately result in more contracts won.

Another benefit of a detailed bid is that you set the customer's expectations for the job. One cause of disputes and the financial consequences they often produce is that the customer has a smaller idea of the job scope than what that scope actually is. Avoid these types of disputes by educating the customer up front about what the job entails.

Added Confidence

A computer-assisted estimate provides increased confidence that the bid price is correct. It also provides more consistent and accurate historical data for future jobs of the same types. Tapping even a little of its potential will improve your competitiveness and increase your profit margins.

8.3 Pre-Purchase Considerations

Although many software vendors present information on the computer screen in a similar manner, you must consider the following during your consideration process:

Usability. Software should be logical, intuitive, simple to use, flexible, and easy to understand. It should provide an on-screen audit trail to review and modify the take-off at any time.

Flexibility. It should provide the capability of factoring labor and/or material cost for every line of the take-off to reflect diverse installation conditions. You should be able to view or change anything in the estimate at any point easily and quickly.

Reports. The system should provide for a permanent audit trail that tracks the input. When looking at software options, pay close attention to the types of reports it will allow you to generate. You need reports that support your business processes. Determine what kinds of reports you need before you even look at estimating software.

Integration. Integration with your accounting system. Is that important?

Your Needs. Are you a small contractor just opening your business, or do you have a large company that has been in business for several years? Some software is more suitable for the former while others are more suitable for the latter. Take this into consideration during your search. Remember that you can always move up to a more sophisticated product when sales improve; sometimes even with the same vendor.

Notes

8.4 Hardware Considerations

Do not make the mistake of trying to use an old, outdated computer to run new, supercharged software. Doing so will result in frustration and disappointment. Besides that, you will not receive the most from your investment.

How do you know if the hardware is outdated? If you are spending time waiting for the computer instead of getting work done, you need to upgrade. If the computer is waiting on you instead of the other way around, then the fact that the computer is not very new may not matter. If you have an older computer, be sure the software you are considering will work with the operating system it uses.

Another place computer buyers tend to save money at great cost is including too little random access memory (RAM). Generally, you want as much RAM as the motherboard on a mid-range machine will accept. RAM is not very expensive, and having plenty of it means you tap the hard drive(s) significantly less. Larger capacity drives have come down significantly in cost, and you should purchase the largest hard drive available for your new computer (or very close). You might be surprised at how fast hard drives can become filled with data from your estimating software, electronic drawing files, submittal documents, electronic catalogs, and so on.

An option that power users consider non-optional is a dual hard-drive system. One hard drive has data only, and the other has the operating system and programs. This arrangement has many advantages. On an NT kernel machine (Windows XP and later), for example, both drives are accessed simultaneously and this provides a huge speed boost when working intensely with data (also at boot-up). It makes backups easier, and provides additional opportunities for data protection.

Perhaps the most compelling reason to have a separate data drive is this—if the operating system fails, you can reinstall it without losing your data even if the installation requires wiping out a partition or reformatting the drive.

Do not forget to have an external backup system. The market offers many types of backup systems, some of which are painfully slow. Take the time to research this and select something that people will actually use. A fast external backup system uses hard drives instead of tape. The problem with that arrangement is the hard drive can fail. But, it is not a high-risk problem and there are ways around it (including dual-drive backups, hard-drive arrays, and parallel online storage). You can also backup information up to a remote site using the Internet.

Notes

8.5 Cost of Software

A single-user license for a quality estimating software system costs between $1,500 and $10,000. Multi-user or network versions will cost more, according to how many users need to be licensed. It is tempting to save money on estimating software, rejecting out of hand anything over a certain price level. This kind of cost savings can be expensive. Instead of taking that approach, determine what your current and anticipated needs are and then look at all of the software that meets those needs.

You need to consider all of the estimating software products, not just those with the lowest prices. The saying, "you get what you pay for" applies to software, too. If you have been on a jobsite after lowball competitors have done the work, you understand all too well how this adage applies to electrical work. Do not make the "low-price blindness" mistake in selecting your software. If it does not meet your needs, then the low-priced purchase is a waste of money.

The high-priced software purchase can also waste money. As you look at an increasing number of bells and whistles, you should evaluate those based on your present and anticipated future needs. Do some math to determine the return on investment of the added cost of an optional feature set or a more robust product. With vendors that offer multiple versions or levels of estimating software, evaluate whether or not your data can migrate to an upgraded system later on, should you choose to purchase one of the lower priced versions.

Make your decision based on the value you will receive for your investment and how well it fits your business needs. Do a little research into how you make additions and changes to the included database of parts and assemblies, and do a ballpark calculation of the time that might be required.

8.6 Technical Support

Software is not a one-time expense; it carries a continuous cost for annual support. Be sure you can count on long-term service from the company and that they will give you close personal attention.

Verify the costs for customer support and the hours they are available for phone and/or e-mail support. If you are going to have multiple systems or have a multi-user network version, find out if it will be a single location annual fee, or if the fee will be "per seat." These fees and services can cost as much as a single-user license but can pay for themselves over the course of a year, especially when a technician helps you restore a job file an hour before a bid is due.

Notes

Before buying a computer-based estimating system, ask the manufacturer for a list of their users, then follow up by calling a few and asking how satisfied they are. Be sure to talk to at least one user who is similar in size to your company and who does work similar to yours.

8.7 Can I Afford it?

In today's world, it is highly unlikely you can be competitive if you estimate without the right software tools. The question is not whether you can afford the right system, but whether you can afford not to have adequate tools for estimating jobs in this competitive environment.

To determine the dollars required in sales to cover the purchase of estimating software, use the following formula:

Sales Increase Required per Year = Software Cost/Gross Profit Percent

Example: *How much must sales increase per year to cover the cost of an estimating system, based on the following factors? It includes software, computer, and training—$6,000; gross profit margin of 40 percent, with expected life of four years.*

Sales = Cost per Year/Gross Profit Percent
Cost per Year = $6,000/4 years
Cost per Year = $1,500
Sales Required per Year = $1,500/40%
Sales Increase Required per Year = $3,750

Notes

Small Contractor Income Statement Year Ending December 31		
Sales	$250,000	100% of Sales
Direct Job Cost		
Labor (4,000 Hrs)	$80,000	
Material	$70,000	
Total Direct Cost	$150,000	60% of Sales
Gross Profit	$100,000	40% of Sales
Overhead Expenses (Administrative Cost)		
Salaries and Commissions	$15,000	
Advertising	$5,000	
Auto and Gas	$10,000	
Benefits	$20,000	
Interest	$1,000	
Insurance—Auto, General, Workers' Comp.	$5,000	
Miscellaneous Expense	$3,000	
Payroll Taxes	$8,000	
Rent	$5,000	
Utilities/Phone	$3,000	
Total Administrative Expenses (50% of Prime)	$75,000	30% of Sales
Net Profit Before Taxes (16.67% of Prime)	**$25,000**	**10% of Sales**

8.8 Software Vendors

Because of the technical nature of electrical estimating, the software for it is not available in computer stores. Only someone who has been trained in electrical contracting can adequately explain how a particular estimating software program works, and discuss with you how it does or does not fit your needs.

Find out as much as you can about the software vendor. How long have they been in the business of selling software? How many customers do they have? What other software products do they sell? What is their background in estimating and electrical contracting? Do not become too excited; take the time to investigate different vendors and make a selection based on facts, not opinions. If possible, see if you can use the software on a trial basis. This might cost you a few hundred dollars so insist on a money back guarantee.

Notes

Author's Comment: Visit www.MikeHolt.com and click on our "Estimating Software" link. There you will find links to all of the major software companies.

8.9 Training and Support

Regardless of how well estimating software is designed, do not expect optimum results without complete training. Professional training requires time away from the office. Attempting to have training in your office during business hours is usually a fiasco due to interruptions from other employees, phone calls, and unexpected visitors.

Be prepared to devote serious time to learning how to use this new tool. It will be extremely difficult to learn to use new software at the same time you are trying to estimate multiple projects. Instead, try to devote extra hours of training after work or on the weekends; the more time you put into using the program, the faster you will master it.

During your negotiations with the vendor, ask if they will provide the training necessary at no additional cost. Some will do so, others will not, but it never hurts to ask!

WARNING: *If you attempt to use your software without proper training, you may never learn all of the valuable features that are designed within the program. Worse, you are likely to set things up in ways that will work against you, and you will probably establish bad practices from the outset. Avoid those problems by knowing what you are doing before you get knee deep into using this new tool.*

8.10 Pricing Services

To most effectively use estimating software, you need to subscribe to a Material Pricing Service to gain assurance that you have current material prices. These programs interface with most major estimating software programs and price almost all of the individual material items in the database.

If you do decide to use a pricing service, be sure you select one whose prices are broken down by geographical area, so that they will more accurately reflect prices where your job is located. Also, just as you checked the background of companies offering estimating software, you should inquire as to the background of companies offering pricing services. Where do they obtain their material prices? What is their relationship to the electrical industry?

If you decide you do not want to use a pricing service, you will most likely need to create material reports for your vendors to price out every estimate you do. This may add to your workload and will make you dependent on your vendors for service. Check with your electrical distributor and key vendors to see what pricing services they provide as well.

The best of pricing services will fail to do the job if the database is not maintained and current. This is a highly responsible chore and should only be assigned to experienced estimators. The database must be secured so that only an authorized person can make revisions. It may be further enhanced to include prices of materials from your suppliers. Some suppliers also provide material prices for items from their database with proprietary stock or catalog numbers. This type of database may not include all the material required by the estimate and may limit seeking competitive material prices.

Keep in mind that pricing services cannot keep up with the constantly changing conduit and wire prices, so you must check the prices for these items for each bid, especially when large quantities are included in the estimate.

Notes

8.11 Frequently Asked Questions

What About Creating My Own Spreadsheet System?

You can do this, but it will be like sending a motor, pulleys, and related parts to a jobsite and telling the foreman to build a wire puller: he will get it done but does it make economic sense? Such an approach will ultimately cost you more than what you will spend by investing in the right software package.

The spreadsheet method can become overwhelmingly complex as you try to scale upward. With an estimating software package, you have many advantages over the homegrown spreadsheet approach. To see these advantages, ask an estimating sales representative to take you on a test drive of their product.

Spreadsheets may be appropriate for Unit Pricing or change orders.

How Do I Handle Take-Offs?

Manual Take-Off. First, you complete the take-off, writing all count and take-off information on a spreadsheet (paper or electronic), then you enter that information into the estimating software.

Direct Take-Off. This method involves entering the count and take-off information directly into the estimating software as you go. When mastered, this step-saving method is a huge time-saver, and it improves accuracy and cuts your chances of making mistakes in half by eliminating the need to write the count and take-off information on a spreadsheet.

Notes

How Much Time Can I Save?

The amount of time saved depends on the software, the estimator, and the complexity of the jobs being estimated. As the estimator becomes more familiar with the system, efficiency improves and the time to do a given task decreases. The more complicated the job, the more the software can save you time by removing grunt work.

As a general rule, once you are proficient with the software, you should be able to complete a computerized estimate in 25 percent of the time that it will take you to do one manually.

Does Software Improve My Accuracy?

Remember, a computer does not make mistakes, it does not get tired, it does not forget the data when distractions occur, it does not omit steps in calculations, and it does not make errors in overlooking taxes, overhead, or profit.

Software can help improve accuracy quite a bit, particularly during the extension phase of your estimates. But if you do not enter the data for your estimate accurately, you will not have an accurate bid.

Will My Estimates Be as Complete?

If you succeed in accurate control and entry, your estimates should be more complete than any done manually. They will also supply information to increase efficiency, and will impress your customers and improve profit margins.

Must I Change My Methods of Estimating?

Yes, to a degree. Most software will be flexible and adapt to your estimating style, but do not expect it to fit all of your needs perfectly.

How Long Will it Take to Become Proficient?

Just as it takes time for an electrician to become a journeyman and then a master electrician, so it takes time to reach advanced levels of proficiency with estimating software. How quickly you increase your proficiency depends on how good an estimator you already are and the amount of time you invest in learning the software. If you do feel frustrated along the way, just relax and try to think through what the designer intended.

Summary

CHAPTER 8

Notes

Introduction

It is important to remember that estimating software is a tool, and cannot by itself ensure your success. It allows estimators to improve accuracy, consistency, and speed when preparing estimates. Estimating software does have its limits. It cannot replace your judgment or experience nor can it replace your knowledge of electrical installations or of the particular installation for which you are preparing an estimate.

8.1 Computer Estimating System Functions

Take-Off. A standard computer-assisted estimating system requires the estimator to take the time to learn how it works and, in addition, requires effort to build the right items or assemblies in the database.

Most systems will have a database of parts and assemblies included in the software product, but someone must take time to verify the assemblies, material prices, and labor units. Once verified, a well setup database can increase the speed and accuracy of the take-off.

Extensions. With estimating software, the extension phase becomes a simple mouse click or two. The computer does the rest with more accuracy and speed than any human (or even a large group of humans) ever could. If something changes or a mistake is found, it is much easier to make the necessary corrections and redo the extensions.

8.2 Advantages and Benefits

Estimating software does not eliminate the need to learn how to estimate. Using software can make a good estimator far more effective. An unskilled estimator is still going to do a poor job of estimating, regardless of whether estimating software is used or not. Advantages and benefits of using software include:

- Better Use of Your Time
- Better Control of Material Cost
- Better Project Management
- Reduced Overhead
- Increased Profitability for Your Business
- Added Confidence

Notes

8.3 Pre-Purchase Considerations

Consider the following factors when deciding on which estimating software to purchase:

- Usability
- Flexibility
- Reports
- Integration
- Your Needs

8.4 Hardware Considerations

Do not make the mistake of trying to use an old, outdated computer to run new, supercharged software. Doing so will result in frustration and disappointment. Besides that, you will not receive the most from your investment.

Another place computer buyers tend to save money at great cost is including too little random access memory (RAM). Generally, you want as much RAM as the motherboard on a mid-range machine will accept. Larger capacity drives have come down significantly in cost, and you should purchase the largest hard drive available for your new computer (or very close).

An option that power users consider non-optional is a dual hard-drive system. One hard drive has data only, and the other has the operating system and programs. Perhaps the most compelling reason to have a separate data drive is this—if the operating system fails, you can reinstall it without losing your data even if the installation requires wiping out a partition or reformatting the drive.

Do not forget to have an external backup system. A fast external backup system uses hard drives instead of tape, or you can back information up to a remote site using the Internet.

8.5 Cost of Software

A single-user license for a quality estimating software system costs between $1,500 and $10,000. Multi-user or network versions will cost more, according to how many users need to be licensed. Determine what your current and anticipated future needs are and then look at all of the software that meets those needs.

Do some math to determine the return on investment of the added cost of an optional feature set or a more robust product. With vendors that offer multiple versions or levels of estimating software, evaluate whether or not your data can migrate to an upgraded system later on, should you choose to purchase one of the lower-priced versions.

Make your decision based on the value you will receive for your investment and how well it fits your business needs. Do a little research into how you make additions and changes to the included database of parts and assemblies, and do a ballpark calculation of the time that might be required.

Notes

8.6 Technical Support

Software is not a one-time expense; it carries a continuous cost for annual support. Be sure you can count on long-term service from the company and that they will give you close personal attention.

Verify the costs for customer support and the hours they are available for phone and/or e-mail support. If you are going to have multiple systems or have a multi-user network version, find out if it will be a single location annual fee, or if the fee will be "per seat."

Before buying a computer-based estimating system ask, the manufacturer for a list of their users, then follow up by calling a few and asking how satisfied they are. Be sure to talk to at least one user who is similar in size to your company and who does work similar to yours.

8.7 Can I Afford it?

In today's world, it is highly unlikely you can be competitive if you estimate without the right software tools. The question is not whether you can afford the right system, but whether you can afford not to have adequate tools for estimating jobs in this competitive environment.

8.8 Software Vendors

Because of the technical nature of electrical estimating, the software for it is not available in computer stores. Only someone who has been trained in electrical contracting can adequately explain how a particular estimating software program works, and discuss with you how it does or does not fit your needs.

8.9 Training and Support

Regardless of how well estimating software is designed, do not expect optimum results without complete training. Professional training requires time away from the office. Be prepared to devote serious time to learning how to use this new tool. Try to devote extra hours of training after work or on the weekends; the more time you put into using the program, the faster you will master it.

Notes

8.10 Pricing Services

To most effectively use estimating software, you need to subscribe to a Material Pricing Service to gain assurance that you have current material prices. These programs interface with most major estimating software programs and price almost all of the individual material items in the database. Be sure you select one whose prices are broken down by geographical area, so that they will more accurately reflect prices where your job is located.

Keep in mind that pricing services cannot keep up with the constantly changing conduit and wire prices, so you must check the prices for these items for each bid, especially when large quantities are included in the estimate.

CHAPTER 8

Conclusion

Notes

This chapter described general considerations about computer-assisted estimating for electrical construction firms. Topics covered included:

- Myths and truths about computer-assisted estimating
- Advantages and benefits of computer-assisted estimating
- Selecting the right estimating software
- Time and effort required to master computer-assisted estimating
- Subscription pricing services used with computer-assisted estimating
- Frequently asked questions about computer-assisted estimating

Computer-assisted estimating can provide the electrical contractor with great benefits by increasing the accuracy of estimates and reducing the time required to compile them. The biggest downfall may still be the accuracy of estimator entries. The old computer industry adage of "Garbage In-Garbage Out" certainly applies to computerized estimating, so exercise extreme caution in all estimating entry steps.

It should also be painfully clear to you by now that a computer with Internet access including e-mail and a Website, and computer-assisted estimating software, have become necessities rather than luxuries.

CHAPTER

8

Essay Questions

Notes

1. What are some things that estimating software cannot replace?

2. What does a standard computer-assisted estimating system require of the estimator?

3. What are some of the advantages and benefits of using estimating software?

4. What factors should be considered when deciding which estimating software to purchase?

5. What are some of the things that should be taken into consideration when purchasing hardware?

6. When considering the cost of software, how should you make your decision?

7. What should you do to ensure the estimating software vendor is reputable and will provide long-term technical support and service?

Notes

8. Why is electrical estimating software not available in computer stores?

9. What is the best way to obtain optimum results from estimating software?

10. What is the most effective way to use estimating software?

11. If you decide to use a pricing service, why should you select one whose prices are broken down by geographical area?

CHAPTER 8

Multiple-Choice Questions

Notes

8.1 Computer Estimating System Functions

1. A standard computer-assisted estimating system requires the estimator to take the time to learn how it works and, in addition, requires _____.

   (a) you to double-check prices
   (b) effort to build the right material items and assemblies in the database
   (c) attention to mathematical functions
   (d) you to enter each material item

2. Once verified, a well setup database can increase the speed and accuracy of the _____.

   (a) specifications checklist
   (b) estimate
   (c) proposal
   (d) take-off

3. A "count entry" function requires typing in and/or clicking a button for the correct value and can be more work than handwriting a symbol or note and then placing a figure underneath it.

   (a) True
   (b) False

8.2 Advantages and Benefits

4. Estimating software does not eliminate the need to _____.

   (a) apply overhead
   (b) apply profit
   (c) learn how to estimate
   (d) calculate extensions

5. Estimating software reduces estimating _____, partly because you no longer need to price, labor, extend, or total material and labor manually.

(a) time
(b) costs
(c) overhead
(d) a and b

6. Once the take-off is complete and you have entered the quantities, you can easily generate a report of all the _____ required for the job.

(a) material
(b) direct costs
(c) labor burden
(d) special conditions

7. A project manager can make a few mouse clicks to update the _____ in real time.

(a) Work Breakdown Structure
(b) Critical Path
(c) Gant Chart
(d) all of these

8. The ability of an estimator to bid more jobs in the same amount of time reduces estimating costs relative to _____.

(a) overhead
(b) profit
(c) labor burden
(d) revenue

9. When you submit a sufficiently detailed bid, you give your customers more reason to be confident in your _____ knowledge of their projects and ability to complete those projects in a timely and competent manner.

(a) company's
(b) employees'
(c) management team's
(d) project manager's

Notes

Notes

10. Another benefit of a detailed bid is that you set the ______ expectations for the job.

    (a) inspector's
    (b) project manager's
    (c) customer's
    (d) employees'

8.3 Pre-Purchase Considerations

11. Software should be logical, intuitive, simple to use, inflexible, and easy to understand.

    (a) True
    (b) False

12. Software should provide the capability of factoring labor and/or material cost for every line of the take-off to reflect ______ installation conditions.

    (a) your
    (b) standard
    (c) diverse
    (d) none of these

13. When looking at software options, pay close attention to the types of reports it will allow you to generate.

    (a) True
    (b) False

8.4 Hardware Considerations

14. Using an old, outdated computer to run new, super-charged software will result in ______.

    (a) slow response time and paper jams in the printer
    (b) frustration and disappointment
    (c) the software making errors
    (d) all of these

8.5 Cost of Software

Notes

15. A single-user license for a quality estimating software system costs between _____.

(a) $1,500 and $10,000
(b) $2,000 and $10,500
(c) $2,500 and $15,000
(d) $3,000 and $15,500

16. Make your decision based on the value you will receive for your investment and how _____.

(a) many features it has
(b) fast it is
(c) many people can use it at the same time
(d) well it fits your business needs

8.6 Technical Support

17. Verify the _____ customer support and the hours they are available for phone and/or e-mail support.

(a) availability of
(b) need for
(c) costs for
(d) reliability of

8.7 Can I Afford It?

18. To determine the dollars required in sales to cover the purchase of estimating software, use the following formula: _____.

(a) Sales Increase Required per Year = Software Cost/Net Profit Percent
(b) Sales Increase Required per Month = Software Cost/Net Profit Percent
(c) Sales Increase Required per Year = Software Cost/Gross Profit Percent
(d) Sales Increase Required per Month = Software Cost/Gross Profit Percent

Notes

8.8 Software Vendors

19. Only someone who has been trained in _____ contracting can adequately explain how a particular estimating software program works, and discuss with you how it does or does not fit your needs.

 (a) general
 (b) electrical
 (c) technical
 (d) architectural

8.9 Training and Support

20. Regardless of how well estimating software is designed, do not expect optimum results without _____.

 (a) technical support
 (b) a user's manual
 (c) complete training
 (d) a telephone

8.10 Pricing Services

21. To most effectively use _____, you need to subscribe to a Material Pricing Service to gain assurance that you have current material prices.

 (a) reports generated by an estimating software program
 (b) worksheets generated by an estimating software program
 (c) estimating software
 (d) none of these

22. If you do decide to use a pricing service, be sure you select one whose prices are broken down by _____.

 (a) geographical area
 (b) material item
 (c) area code
 (d) labor hours

CHAPTER 9 THE BID PROCESS REVIEW

INTRODUCTION

We have discussed many concepts and pitfalls to consider when estimating (and bidding) a job. You may be feeling rather overwhelmed at this point but you now have the knowledge you need to prepare an accurate estimate. You have learned the importance of:

- Prequalifying requests for bids to decide if you want to do the job.
- Accurately determining all of your costs to reach the break-even point.
- How to determine your Estimated Prime Cost.
- Properly applying overhead and profit.
- Items that should be addressed in your proposal.
- Checking for accuracy.
- Performing analyses on your bids.

This chapter essentially summarizes the steps that should be taken whenever you receive a request to provide a customer a price for work to be completed. Use it as a quick reference as you master the science, and the art, of estimating.

9.1 Pre-Estimate

Job Selection (Step 1 [4.1])

Pre-Bid Checklist. Because there is always a limit to your energy, time, and money, you cannot estimate all jobs that are presented to you. So before estimating any job, ask yourself a few questions:

- Am I qualified to estimate this project?
- Are the contractor and/or owner's scheduling expectations realistic?
- Can I make money on this job?
- Can I manage this job so that it is profitable?
- Do I have enough time to properly estimate this job?
- Do I have the financial resources for this job?
- Do I have the proper tools and equipment to complete this job with profit?
- Do I have the workforce to handle this job?

Notes

- Do I want the job?
- Do I want to work with this person or organization?
- Do we have the skills to do this job effectively?
- What is the likelihood of winning the job if my price is competitive?
- What risk does this job present for our company?
- What does my gut say about this project or the contractor and/or owner?
- Will I be competitive?

Just Say No! You do not have to bid every job offered, just the ones that you believe you have a chance of winning while maintaining a profit margin that meets you needs. If you have decided that you are not interested in bidding a given job, immediately communicate this to the appropriate individual and remain firm in your decision.

Financial Resources. Only bid jobs where the anticipated cash flow (you might not get paid on time) provides the funds you need for payroll, material, and overhead.

Listen to Your Gut Feelings. You cannot always prove that something is wrong. However, proof is not always necessary to know that you should not take a certain job. Make it a practice to only work for customers you like and who respect you and your staff.

Before you expend any energy estimating a job, do some research on the individual or company; run a credit check and talk with other trades about their reputation for paying bills in a timely manner. Ask who did their electrical work in the past and try to determine why he or she wants to make a change.

Understanding the Scope of Work (Step 2 [4.2])

Once you have decided to bid the job, but before you begin, learn everything you can about the scope of the work to be completed according to the complete set of drawings and specifications.

Plans (Working Drawings). Be sure that you receive all of the pages of the drawings. Review all notes on other trade drawings for items that may have an impact on the electrical work, including architectural floor and ceiling drawings, architectural elevation drawings, mechanical drawings, and structural drawings. The first thing to do when you receive them is to make sure they are legible and clear; then verify that you have a full set.

Specifications. Written specifications are additional requirements that govern the material to be used and the work to be performed. Specifications are designed to simplify the task of interpreting the drawings. They should clear up many issues, but they can also add to (or conflict with) the drawings. Be sure to review all sections of the project for work that may be assigned to the electrical contractor. Specifications are a part of the "contract bidding documents" and must be considered in your bids.

Notes

Visit the Jobsite. Be sure to visit the jobsite before you bid the job. Some electrical contractors use a video and/or digital camera to document the jobsite conditions in an effort to reduce errors with the estimate and prove their visit to the site. This is especially important when doing remodel work as the pictures will remind you of details you may have forgotten. At the very least, be sure to write down what you discover during your site visit.

Preparing for the Estimate (Step 3 [4.3])

You need to create a job folder in which to put your bid notes, job information sheet, take-off worksheets, bill-of-material worksheets, quote sheets, summary sheet, and other papers associated with the estimate. This folder should also include the Estimate Record Worksheet which is a form containing pertinent job information, such as the job name, job location and address, telephone numbers, names of the owner, general contractor, architect, engineer, and to whom the bid is to be submitted.

Plans and Specifications Review (Step 4 [4.4])

Carefully read the specifications document and all notes on the drawings so that you have a clear understanding of the scope of the project and the bid requirements before you begin the actual take-off. Review legends, details, notations, and symbols. Become familiar with the entire installation and check for any special or unusual features such as elevated ceilings.

To help you keep track of the drawings and specifications details, complete the Specifications Checklist worksheet as you proceed through the estimate. Create a checklist of important items to be checked off when the estimate is near completion.

Estimate and Bid Notes (Step 5 [4.5])

Keep a notepad (or electronic text file) handy and write down any questions you have as you proceed through the estimate. If there is anything that is unclear, get the answer as soon as possible—do not wait until the last minute.

Keep a request for information (RFI) log and include this with your proposal.

Using e-mails instead of the telephone is significantly faster, and they create a documentation trail. If you use the phone, make sure you write down the answer to your question on the notepad (or the electronic file) when you receive it. If you do not receive satisfactory answers to your questions, then you are left with a difficult decision—bid the job and list the exclusions in your proposal, or do not bid the job at all. Follow up the phone call with an e-mail noting key details, "Per our conversation today, the following will be included in my proposal."

Notes

Estimating Forms and Worksheets (Step 6 [4.6])

To quickly and accurately estimate a job, use proper estimating forms and worksheets to save time, create consistency, and help reduce errors. They also help serve as a reminder of items that are easily omitted or forgotten.

Different types of construction, lend themselves to different types of estimating forms or worksheets. In addition, different types of forms and worksheets are required for different parts of the estimate. You can use a computer to design custom worksheets or order them from places like Minnesota Electrical Association.

9.2 Estimate Process

The Take-Off (Step 1 [4.7])

A take-off is the action of counting symbols and measuring lengths that we will later use to determine the bill-of-material. A proper take-off ensures there will be little need to refer to the drawings or specifications to complete the estimate. To accomplish this, you must follow an orderly, organized, methodical routine that is complete and consistent for each and every job.

- **General.** Use colored pencils, pens, or highlighters to identify each item that you have taken off. When you have finished the take-off, your drawings should be a colored representation of the electrical work that needs to be installed. If you are not permitted to mark up the paper drawings, then you need make a full size copy.
- **Counting**. The purpose of counting symbols is to ascertain and record the quantities of a given electrical component like fixtures, switches, receptacles, and so on, that will be required on the job.
- **Measuring**. Measuring consists of determining the circuit length for branch circuits, feeders, and service raceways or cables.

Determining the Bill-of-Material (Step 2 [4.8])

Once the take-off is complete, the next step is to determine the bill-of-material, which means determining the type, size, and quantity of all material items required to complete the installation.

Determining the bill-of-material requires the estimator to have the ability to visualize all of the material items needed for each symbol. If you do not understand the electrical wiring requirements or do not have that visualization ability, you cannot determine the bill-of-material.

Notes

- **Material Spreadsheet.** Manual estimates require the bill-of-material to be extracted from the take-off in the most efficient manner, which is with the use of a spreadsheet.

Pricing and Laboring (Step 3 [4.9])

After developing the bill-of-material, you need to transfer the items and their quantities to the Price/Labor Worksheet for pricing and laboring.

Extensions and Totals (Step 4 [4.10])

After penciling in the material cost and the labor-hour value for each item, you must determine the material cost and labor-hour extensions for them, then calculate the totals for each worksheet page.

9.3 Determining Break-Even Cost

Once your bid price covers all of your job costs (the break-even point), every dollar above that is a dollar of profit, but every dollar below it is a dollar of loss.

- Add the cost of labor, material, direct job expenses, and overhead together.

It is worth noting that one mistake in calculating the break-even point can be costly. Throughout the break-even analysis process, you will have to make judgment decisions on intangibles, such as job conditions, labor productivity, material requirements, waste, theft, small tools, direct job expenses, and overhead.

Labor Hours (Step 1 [5.1])

The first step in determining your break-even cost is to transfer the labor hours and material cost from the Price/Labor Worksheets to the Estimate Summary Worksheet.

Labor-Unit Adjustments. The estimated labor hours must be adjusted for working conditions based on a percentage of the total (or fixed) man-hours for specific conditions. Determining labor adjustments comes with experience and is part of what makes estimating an art form.

Additional Labor. After you have adjusted the total labor-unit hours, you must consider any additional labor requirements for the job that might apply. Be aware that these conditions are not adjustments of the labor unit for job conditions, but additional labor that might be required, such as:

Notes

- As-Built Drawings
- Demolition
- Environmentally Hazardous Material Disposal
- Excavation, Trenching, and Backfill
- Job Location
- Jobsite Meetings
- Match-Up of Existing Equipment
- Miscellaneous Material Items
- Mobilization and Demobilization
- Nonproductive Labor
- Plans and Specifications
- Power
- Public Safety
- Security
- Service and Warranty
- Site Conditions
- Subcontract Supervision
- Training

Labor Cost (Step 2 [5.2])

The estimated labor cost for a job is determined by multiplying the total adjusted labor man-hours by the labor rate per man-hour.

Labor Rate per Man-Hour (Step 3 [5.3])

The labor rate per man-hour can be determined by one of two methods: the shop average, or the job average.

Labor Burden (Step 4 [5.4])

In addition to the cost of labor, there are other costs associated with labor that must be taken into consideration. These include employer paid Social Security and Medicare taxes, Workers' Compensation insurance, as well as employee benefits. These costs are identified as "labor burden" costs.

Labor burden expenses are generally listed in the income statement under overhead. When this occurs, labor burden will be applied to the estimate when overhead is applied.

Notes

Material Cost (Step 5 [5.5])

The second step in determining your break-even cost is to transfer the material cost from the Price/Labor Worksheets to the Estimate Summary Worksheet. Once this is accomplished, you will need to account for lighting fixtures and switch gear, miscellaneous material, sales tax, small tools, and waste and theft.

Direct Job Expenses (Step 6 [5.6])

Step three in determining the break-even cost is to account for direct job expenses which are often not shown on the drawings, but probably indicated in the specifications. Direct job costs include:

- Allowances and Contingencies
- Business and Occupational Fees
- Coordination Drawings
- Engineering/Working Drawings
- Equipment/Rental
- Job Insurance/Bond
- OSHA Compliance (Safety Equipment)
- Out-of-Town Expenses
- Parking Fees
- Permits and Inspection Fees
- Public Safety
- Recycling Fees
- Storage
- Temporary Power
- Testing and Certification Fees
- Trash Disposal
- Utility Charges and Fees

Estimated Prime Cost (Step 7 [5.7])

"Estimated Prime Cost" is simply a term used to identify the subtotaled cost of labor, material, and direct costs. The term allows us to clearly identify the number to which overhead is to be applied. Calculating your estimated prime cost is just the simple matter of adding up the costs of labor, material, and direct job costs.

Notes

Overhead (Step 8 [5.8 and 5.9])

The cost related to the operation and management of the company such as rent, insurance, vehicles, administrative salaries, professional fees, and so on is known as "overhead" and is usually obtained from your income statement or your accountant.

- As business volume increases, the cost of overhead per labor hour decreases.
- Smaller jobs/contractors have a higher overhead cost to labor as compared to larger jobs/contractors.

There are two methods of applying overhead to a job:

- Percentage to prime cost
- Rate per labor-hour

The percentage method is only suitable when it is being used on similar jobs where the ratio of material cost to labor cost is approximately the same from job to job. Since overhead is related primarily to the management of labor and not the cost of material, it should be applied to the labor man-hours of a job. Overhead per man-hour is calculated by dividing overhead dollars for a given period of time, by the actual field man-hours for the same period of time.

9.4 The Bid Process

Applying Profit (Step 1)

High bids can cause you to lose the sales that your company depends on. Low bids can win sales, but cause the loss of profits or the demise of the company. Between these two losing propositions is the "accurate" bid—and that is the only kind of bid you want to produce.

The accurate bid:

- Helps lock in profits.
- Eliminates built-in loss of revenue or profit.
- Provides a means for knocking low bids out of the competition.
- Reduces cash-flow problems.
- Reduces resource conflicts.
- Provides the highest return on the bidding effort.
- Provides accurate information for negotiation to win a job or support changes.
- Reduces risk.

Notes

It is important that you understand what a "winning bid" actually is. It is one of two things:

- It lands you a profitable job that your company can handle.
- It prevents you from taking on a losing project.

A losing bid is one of two things:

- It prevents you from taking on a profitable project that your company can handle because the bid was too high.
- It lands you a losing project because the bid was too low.

Net profit is the bottom line; what all business persons are measured against. A winning bid includes a reasonable amount for profit. A reasonable profit margin will be whatever the market will bear without gouging the customer. Some factors to consider include:

- Competition and the Economy
- Management/Organization
- Job Size
- Risk
- Speed of Payment

Most contractors apply profit as a percentage of break-even cost, so be sure to use a markup multiplier, not the percent of profit to sales value from the financial statement!

Other Bid Cost Considerations (Step 2 [6.3])

Be sure you review the plans and specifications one final time before submitting your bid, and make sure you understand all of the bid conditions, such as:

- Completion Penalty
- Finance Cost
- Liquidated Damages
- Retainage Cost

Bid Accuracy (Step 3 [6.4])

To ensure that your bid is accurate, you need to verify that you have not made any of the following errors:

- Assuming standard-grade devices, when specification grade is required
- Errors in math or calculations
- Failure to review jobsite conditions, especially for retrofit jobs

Notes

- Failure to comply with specifications or drawing notes
- Forgetting a major item, such as a switchgear or subcontractor quote
- Forgetting to include outside or underground work
- Not transferring totals properly from page to page
- Omitting a section of the estimate, like an entire floor
- Using improper estimating forms that lead to errors
- Using supplier take-off quantities for quotes
- Relying on verbal supplier quotes
- Not verifying that quotes (for example fixtures or switchgear) match the schedules or specifications
- Using the wrong scale on reduced size drawings
- Using the wrong labor unit
- Using the wrong material cost

Bid Analysis (Step 4 [6.5])

Before you submit your bid to the customer, do as much bid analysis as you can to ensure that your bid is as accurate as possible and that nothing fell through the cracks. Types of analyses include:

- Average Branch Raceway Length per Outlet
- Average Number of Wires per Raceway Foot
- Percent Distribution to Selling Price
- Cost per Square Foot
- Cost per Labor Hour
- Labor Days

Bid Proposal (Step 5 [6.6])

When the bid is complete, you must submit a written proposal that clarifies what the bid includes and what it does not.

FINAL EXAM

1.1 Estimating versus Bidding

1. The purpose of ______ is to determine the cost of a project before you actually do the work.

    (a) negotiating
    (b) bidding
    (c) estimating
    (d) selling

2. Once you know the estimated cost of a project, you add ______ to determine the selling (bid) price of the job.

    (a) overhead
    (b) profit
    (c) labor burden
    (d) none of these

1.3 Objectives and Purpose of an Electrical Contractor

3. The purpose of an electrical contractor is to ______.

    (a) stay in business
    (b) determine the cost of every job offered
    (c) treat employees fairly
    (d) make a profit on every single job

4. The first step to becoming a successful electrical contractor is to determine your ______.

    (a) overhead
    (b) expected cost
    (c) profit margin
    (d) labor burden

Notes

1.5 Project Management

5. The factor(s) pertaining to the ultimate cost of a project is(are) ______.

   (a) effective job planning
   (b) labor scheduling
   (c) material purchasing
   (d) all of these

1.6 Can I Be Competitive?

6. When possible, try not to bid jobs that have more than ______ competitors.

   (a) four
   (b) five
   (c) six
   (d) seven

7. ______ is(are) an important ingredient(s) in having your price accepted.

   (a) Professionalism
   (b) Confidence
   (c) a or b
   (d) a and b

1.7 The Electrical Market

8. Consider every ______ as an opportunity to monitor the market's direction, and then decide which path you will choose to follow.

   (a) bid request
   (b) telephone call
   (c) completed estimate
   (d) all of these

Notes

2.2 Duties and Responsibilities of the Estimator

9. Besides determining the cost of the job, the electrical estimator is often responsible for ______.

   (a) material purchases
   (b) project management information and tracking
   (c) a and b
   (d) none of these

2.3 The Estimating Workspace and Tools

10. Before you even think of estimating a job, you need to have ______.

    (a) the proper workspace
    (b) the proper tools
    (c) appropriate lighting
    (d) all of these

11. Proper estimating tools ______.

    (a) reduce human errors
    (b) increase efficiency
    (c) quickly pay for themselves
    (d) all of these

2.4 Types of Bids

12. In ______ bidding, the lowest price is sought for a project in a bidding process.

    (a) negotiated
    (b) design/build
    (c) competitive
    (d) time and material

13. Some jobs are awarded on the basis of unit pricing (price to install a given electrical component) where the unit price includes the cost of labor, material, overhead, and profit.

    (a) True
    (b) False

Notes

2.6 Improper Estimating Methods

14. Thinking that "you will get away without including a requirement" from the _____ is not a good strategy if you plan on staying in business.

(a) plans
(b) specifications
(c) a and b
(d) a or b

15. The estimating method that makes a great way to badger the customer to death for additional money once everyone's committed and the job is under way is called "_____."

(a) ignoring errors in the prints and specifications
(b) meeting the lowest bid
(c) the "Shot-in-the-Dark" method
(d) all of these

2.7 The Detailed Estimating Method

16. Read all of the specifications and make notes of the items that affect the cost. Complete a _____ so you will know when the estimate is done.

(a) job folder
(b) checklist
(c) worksheet
(d) none of these

17. A(n) "_____" is the process of counting and measuring to determine the material needed for the project.

(a) estimate
(b) bid
(c) take-off
(d) bill-of-material

18. Information gathered from the _____ is used to create the _____ required for the project.

(a) take-off, estimate
(b) bid, bill-of-material
(c) bill-of-material, take-off
(d) take-off, bill-of material

19. Once you have determined the total cost for material and the total labor hours needed, you must apply labor burden.

(a) True
(b) False

20. Applying the correct values for ______ is where many contractors fail.

(a) overhead
(b) profit
(c) other final costs
(d) all of these

2.8 How Accurate Can an Estimate Be?

21. As an estimator, you cannot control variables such as ______.

(a) productivity
(b) cost of material
(c) the activities of other trades
(d) all of these

22. A material budget must be given to the ______ to ensure the job is completed as estimated.

(a) general contractor
(b) inspector
(c) job supervisor
(d) customer

23. Labor is more difficult to predict than material, but with experience, labor can be calculated to within ______ percent for new work, and ______ percent for remodeling jobs.

(a) 5, 15
(b) 10, 20
(c) 15, 25
(d) 20, 30

Notes

Notes

2.9 Manual Estimate, Estimating Software, or an Estimating Service?

24. Manual estimating requires so much ______ that estimates often become backlogged and project management suffers.

    (a) paperwork
    (b) time
    (c) a and b
    (d) none of these

25. ______ is only as good as the person's experience in using the system.

    (a) Manual estimating
    (b) An estimating service
    (c) Computer-assisted estimating
    (d) none of these

26. ______ is a temporary agency that you use and pay for only when you need it.

    (a) Manual estimating
    (b) An estimating service
    (c) Computer-assisted estimating
    (d) none of these

3.1 What Is a Labor Unit?

27. A labor unit represents the approximate amount of time required to install an electrical product, component, or piece of equipment.

    (a) True
    (b) False

28. The systems for a typical project assume electrical service by the utility, new listed material, and not more than ______ feet above a solid floor.

    (a) 10
    (b) 15
    (c) 20
    (d) 25

Notes

29. The site conditions for a typical project assume a minimum temperature of _____, a maximum temperature of _____, and 50 percent relative humidity.

(a) 30ºF, 83ºF
(b) 35ºF, 88ºF
(c) 40ºF, 93ºF
(d) 45ºF, 95ºF

3.3 Using Work Experience

30. Work experience is important, as a matter of fact it is critical, so it should be your basis for estimating a job.

(a) True
(b) False

3.4 What Is Included in the Labor Unit?

31. The actual installation time only represents about _____ percent of the labor unit.

(a) 20
(b) 30
(c) 40
(d) 50

32. The layout of the work represents _____ percent of the labor unit.

(a) 5
(b) 10
(c) 15
(d) 20

33. Material handling and cleanup represents _____ percent of the labor unit.

(a) 5
(b) 10
(c) 15
(d) 20

Notes

34. All jobs include nonproductive labor, which should be managed so as not to exceed _____ percent of the labor unit.

(a) 5
(b) 10
(c) 15
(d) 20

35. Supervision represents _____ percent of the labor unit.

(a) 10
(b) 20
(c) 30
(d) 40

36. The management, handling, and layout of tools represent _____ percent of the labor unit.

(a) 5
(b) 10
(c) 15
(d) 20

3.5 Labor Units Do Not Include

37. Labor units do not include _____.

(a) the assembly of fixtures
(b) equipment supplied by others
(c) a or b
(d) none of these

3.6 Labor-Unit Manuals

38. You must purchase a comprehensive labor-unit manual that contains at least _____ labor units.

(a) 5,000
(b) 10,000
(c) 15,000
(d) 20,000

Notes

3.7 How to Develop Your Own Labor Units

39. You will really not develop your own labor units, what you will develop is the "labor unit _____."

    (a) condition
    (b) quantifier
    (c) average
    (d) adjustment

3.8 Your Labor Units as Compared to Your Competitors

40. Productivity in the installation of electrical equipment is affected by many factors, and the most significant is _____.

    (a) project management
    (b) proper tools
    (c) highly trained, skilled, and motivated electricians
    (d) coordination of the trades

41. Labor units are based on the assumption that _____ electricians are completing the task.

    (a) highly trained
    (b) skilled
    (c) motivated
    (d) all of these

42. To complete a project efficiently, you must have the material and tools, and all pertinent information, on the job _____.

    (a) at all times
    (b) when they are needed
    (c) only when they are available
    (d) none of these

Notes

3.9 Knowing Your Competitors' Labor Units

43. It does not help you to know the labor units your competitors use because _____ is(are) unique to your company.

    (a) your style of management
    (b) your organizational strengths and weaknesses
    (c) the skill of your labor force
    (d) all of these

3.10 Variables That Affect Labor Units

44. Add _____ percent for the single floor level you are working on. For example, if you are doing a build-out on the ninth floor, increase your total labor by _____ percent.

    (a) 1, 9
    (b) 1.50, 13.50
    (c) 2, 18
    (d) 2.50, 22.50

45. Consider applying a labor adjustment of _____ percent for boxes and _____ percent for raceways when that portion of the wiring method will be exposed

    (a) 1, 5
    (b) 5, 15
    (c) 7, 18
    (d) 10, 20

46. Labor-unit adjustments for ladder work should be considered for any portion of the job that is not at grade level, such as _____ percent when working 12 ft above grade.

    (a) 3
    (b) 5
    (c) 8
    (d) 10

Notes

47. Overtime interrupts established life patterns and causes fatigue, reduced motivation, and lower productivity. Consider adjusting all labor hours by _____ percent when your labor force must work six 10-hour days.

    (a) 16
    (b) 17
    (c) 18
    (d) 30

Chapter 4 Introduction

48. Companies do not bid on jobs to get work or revenue, they do so to make a profit and to _____.

    (a) keep their employees busy
    (b) maintain cash flow
    (c) stay in tune with the market conditions
    (d) monitor the competition

4.1 Job Selection

49. You should always try to estimate all jobs that are presented to you.

    (a) True
    (b) False

4.2 Understanding the Scope of Work

50. The first thing to do when you receive the drawings is to be sure _____.

    (a) they are legible
    (b) they are clear
    (c) you have a full set
    (d) all of these

Notes

4.3 Preparing for the Estimate

51. Once you have completed the Estimate Record Worksheet, ______.

(a) keep it handy for future reference
(b) immediately file it in the job folder
(c) make a copy and send it to the customer
(d) none of these

4.4 Plans and Specifications Review

52. Carefully read the specifications document and all notes on the drawings so that you have a clear understanding of the ______ of the project and the bid requirements before you begin the actual take-off.

(a) location
(b) conditions
(c) scope
(d) all of these

53. Become familiar with the ______ and check for any special or unusual features such as elevated ceilings.

(a) plans
(b) job
(c) specifications
(d) entire installation

54. Underline, circle, or highlight important and/or unusual items that can affect the ______.

(a) estimate
(b) bid
(c) job
(d) schedule

55. To help you keep track of the drawings and specifications details, complete the ______ as you proceed through the estimate.

(a) Estimate Record worksheet
(b) Specifications Checklist worksheet
(c) bill-of-material
(d) all of these

Notes

4.5 Estimate and Bid Notes

56. If there is anything that is unclear, get the answer as soon as possible—do not wait until the last minute. Contact the _____, but be sure you have your questions answered as soon as possible.

(a) general contractor or inspector
(b) customer
(c) architect or engineer
(d) none of these

4.6 Estimating Forms and Worksheets

57. To quickly and accurately estimate a job, use proper estimating forms and worksheets to _____.

(a) save time
(b) create consistency
(c) help reduce errors
(d) all of these

4.7 The Take-Off

58. A take-off is the action of counting symbols and measuring lengths that we will later use to determine the _____.

(a) estimate
(b) bid
(c) bill-of-material
(d) proposal

59. A proper take-off ensures there will be little need to refer to the drawings or specifications to complete the _____.

(a) estimate
(b) bid
(c) bill-of-material
(d) proposal

Notes

60. To count symbols accurately, you must be capable of _____ all drawing symbols.

    (a) reading
    (b) interpreting
    (c) a or b
    (d) a and b

61. Measuring consists of determining the circuit length for branch circuits, feeders, and service raceways or cables.

    (a) True
    (b) False

62. When measuring the circuit wiring, _____ the line that represents the wiring with a colored pen or pencil.

    (a) trace
    (b) visualize
    (c) cross out
    (d) dot

63. The three typical take-off sequences include: section at a time, start at service and end with lighting, or start with lighting and end with service.

    (a) True
    (b) False

4.9 Pricing and Laboring

64. If you do not have a cost for a particular material item, _____ so that you know later you did not omit it.

    (a) make a note of it on your note pad
    (b) do not bid the job
    (c) draw a line through the cost field
    (d) guess at the cost

Notes

65. Laboring consists of looking up the labor unit associated with each material item and penciling those values onto the _____.

(a) Price/Labor Worksheet
(b) Estimate Checklist Worksheet
(c) Bill-of-Material Spreadsheet
(d) Specifications Checklist

5.1 Labor Hours

66. Determining labor adjustments comes with experience and is part of what makes estimating _____.

(a) a science
(b) difficult
(c) an art form
(d) easy

67. After you have adjusted the total labor-unit hours, you must consider any additional _____ for the job that might apply.

(a) labor requirements
(b) miscellaneous material
(c) material requirements
(d) none of these

5.2 Labor Cost

68. The actual labor cost for a job is determined by multiplying the total adjusted labor man-hours by the labor rate per man-hour.

(a) True
(b) False

Notes

5.3 Labor Rate per Man-Hour

69. The shop average labor rate per man-hour is determined by ______ the total field labor cost over a given period of time by the total number of field man-hours over the same period of time.

(a) adding
(b) subtracting
(c) multiplying
(d) dividing

70. Another approach in determining the labor rate per man-hour is to use the anticipated ______ labor rate per man-hour.

(a) prevailing
(b) job average
(c) union scale
(d) cheapest possible

5.5 Total Material Cost

71. The second step in determining your break-even cost is to transfer the ______ from the Price/Labor Worksheets to the Estimate Summary Worksheet.

(a) lighting fixtures and switch gear
(b) miscellaneous material
(c) sales tax and small tools
(d) material cost

72. Add a percentage to the total cost of material as an adjustment for miscellaneous material. An addition of ______ percent of the material cost as a factor is suggested when you are doing the estimate manually.

(a) 10
(b) 11
(c) 12
(d) 13

Notes

73. A factor of _____ percent of the total material cost is considered an acceptable value for small tools.

(a) 1
(b) 2
(c) 3
(d) 4

5.6 Direct Job Expenses

74. Step three in determining the break-even cost is to account for _____ expenses which are often not shown on the drawings, but probably indicated in the specifications.

(a) lighting fixtures and switch gear
(b) direct job
(c) sales tax and small tools
(d) profit

5.8 Overhead

75. The cost related to the operation and management of the company such as rent, insurance, vehicles, administrative salaries, professional fees, and so on, is known as "_____."

(a) overhead
(b) profit
(c) labor burden
(d) none of these

5.10 Break-Even Cost (Estimated Cost)

76. To determine the break-even cost, all you need to do is add the cost of labor, material, direct job expenses, overhead, and profit together.

(a) True
(b) False

Notes

6.1 Profit (It Is Not a Dirty Word)

77. A reasonable profit margin will be whatever _____ without gouging the customer.

(a) the market will bear
(b) the customer will accept
(c) management dictates
(d) any of these

78. If the economy is strong or the market is expanding, prices and profits typically _____.

(a) remain stable
(b) decrease
(c) increase
(d) fluctuate

6.3 Other Bid Cost Considerations

79. Be sure you review the plans and specifications one final time before _____, and make sure you understand all of the bid conditions.

(a) submitting your bid
(b) planning your proposal
(c) applying profit and overhead
(d) considering labor burden

6.4 Bid Accuracy

80. To ensure that your bid is accurate, you need to verify that you have not made any of the typical errors.

(a) True
(b) False

Notes

6.5 Bid Analysis

81. Before you ______, do as much bid analysis as you can to ensure that your bid is as accurate as possible and that nothing fell through the cracks.

    (a) prepare the final proposal
    (b) determine your break-even cost
    (c) apply profit
    (d) submit your bid to the customer

82. A quick check worth doing is to ______ the total footage of branch raceways ______ the number of outlets.

    (a) add, to
    (b) subtract, from
    (c) multiply, by
    (d) divide, by

83. Another quick check is to divide branch-circuit wiring by branch raceway lengths. If the answer is less than 2 or more than ______, that is a warning sign to check for errors.

    (a) 3
    (b) 4
    (c) 5
    (d) 6

84. You should also check the percentage distribution of labor, material, direct cost, overhead, and profit to sales.

    (a) True
    (b) False

6.6 Bid Proposal

85. When the bid is complete, you must submit a ______ proposal that clarifies what the bid includes and what it does not.

    (a) verbal
    (b) written
    (c) a or b
    (d) a and b

Notes

7.1 What Is Unit Pricing?

86. Unit pricing consists of developing a(n) _____ price to install a given electrical component.

(a) set
(b) estimated
(c) average
(d) flexible

7.2 Advantages and Disadvantages of Unit Pricing

87. The biggest advantage when using unit pricing is that you do not need to complete a take-off to determine the number of luminaries, switches, receptacles, and so forth.

(a) True
(b) False

88. Unit pricing is not suitable for jobs where outlets are not located at standard intervals.

(a) True
(b) False

8.1 Computer Estimating System Functions

89. A standard computer-assisted estimating system requires the estimator to take the time to learn how it works and, in addition, requires _____.

(a) you to double-check prices
(b) effort to build the right material items and assemblies in the database
(c) attention to mathematical functions
(d) you to enter each material item

90. Once verified, a well setup database can increase the speed and accuracy of the _____.

(a) specifications checklist
(b) estimate
(c) proposal
(d) take-off

Notes

91. A "count entry" function requires typing in and/or clicking a button for the correct value and can be more work than handwriting a symbol or note and then placing a figure underneath it.

(a) True
(b) False

8.2 Advantages and Benefits

92. Estimating software does not eliminate the need to ______.

(a) apply overhead
(b) apply profit
(c) learn how to estimate
(d) calculate extensions

93. Estimating software reduces estimating ______, partly because you no longer need to price, labor, extend, or total material and labor manually.

(a) time
(b) costs
(c) overhead
(d) a and b

94. Once the take-off is complete and you have entered the quantities, you can easily generate a report of all the _____ required for the job.

(a) material
(b) direct costs
(c) labor burden
(d) special conditions

95. A project manager can make a few mouse clicks to update the _____ in real time.

(a) Work Breakdown Structure
(b) Critical Path
(c) Gant Chart
(d) all of these

Notes

96. The ability of an estimator to bid more jobs in the same amount of time reduces estimating costs relative to _____.

(a) overhead
(b) profit
(c) labor burden
(d) revenue

97. When you submit a sufficiently detailed bid, you give your customers more reason to be confident in your _____ knowledge of their projects and ability to complete those projects in a timely and competent manner.

(a) company's
(b) employees'
(c) management team's
(d) project manager's

98. Another benefit of a detailed bid is that you set the _____ expectations for the job.

(a) inspector's
(b) project manager's
(c) customer's
(d) employees'

8.7 Can I Afford It?

99. To determine the dollars required in sales to cover the purchase of estimating software, use the following formula: _____.

(a) Sales Increase Required per Year = Software Cost /Net Profit Percent
(b) Sales Increase Required per Month = Software Cost /Net Profit Percent
(c) Sales Increase Required per Year = Software Cost /Gross Profit Percent
(d) Sales Increase Required per Month = Software Cost /Gross Profit Percent

8.9 Training and Support

100. Regardless of how well estimating software is designed, do not expect optimum results without _____.

(a) technical support
(b) a user's manual
(c) complete training
(d) a telephone